10
REASONS
IGBO PEOPLE ARE
RICH &
SUCCESSFUL
BUSINESS PEOPLE

The Secret of Igbo Economic Power

"*A study of the Igbo-Ukwu finds made by Professor Shaw T. (1970) would seem to reveal that by the ninth century A. D. Igbo land was already engaged in long and short-range exchange business.*"
(Afigbo A. E.)

Humphrey Kanayo Akaolisa

Copyright © 2012 Humphrey Kanayo Akaolisa

+2348024478189

All rights reserved.

ISBN-13:978-1480055643

ISBN-10:1480055646

SECOND EDITION

DEDICATION

To The Memory of My God Father

**His Royal Highness
Late IGWE PATRICK O. OKOLO
(Ochiagha 1 n'Ichida)
An Astute Wealthy Businessman,
A Core Igbo Personality,
& A Great Leader.**

ACKNOWLEDGMENTS

I duly acknowledge all the people and books that offered me great insight from the conception to the conclusion of this work. I wish to make a special appreciation of my literary idol, Chinua Achebe, and my mentor, J. Obi Oguejiofor, whose works on the Igbo personality and cultural traits immensely influenced and inspired this work.

CONTENTS

FOREWORD vii

PREFACE xi

PREFACE II xiii

AUTHOR'S NOTE xiv

INTRODUCTION xvii
The Igbo People of South-Eastern Nigeria
Igbo Influence in Nigeria

1	Igbo Worldview, Adaptability to Change and Cultures Assimilation	1
2	Ancient Trading and Development of Mercantile	13
3	Apprenticeship and Community Consciousness	20
4	Igbo Society Age Grading System and Title Society	26
5	Ambitious, Hardy and Headstrong	32

6	Clannishness, Aggressiveness, Fear and Industry of the Igbo Women	41
7	Hard Work, Faithfulness and Desire for Achievement	50
8	Competitiveness, Confidence and Ability to Take Risks	63
9	Egalitarian Individualism, Managerial Qualities and Astuteness	68
10	Democratic Institutions and Freedom of the Individual	79

CONCLUSIONS — 88

EPILOGUE: — 95
The Traditional Igbo Socio-Political Structure

BIBLIOGRAPHY — 105

GLOSSARY — 111

INDEX — 115

FOREWORD

The book of Ecclesiastes reminds us, in style, what should really be obvious, that there is a season, a time, for everything under the sun – under heaven. For the Igbo, now is the time to make peace – time to make friends – within and without. It is time to unify and integrate. It is time to court the friendship of other Nigerians. For those in Diaspora, or outside Igbo land, it is time to make friends with our host communities. To make peace, to make friends, we need to understand the basis of the attitude of other Nigerians to us (the Igbo). It is not just other Nigerians; indeed, it is the attitude, to us, of other peoples of the world, with whom we come into close relationship. Igbo slaves, in the epoch of slavery and slave trade, were seen and treated differently from other slaves – they attracted higher prices but there were slave masters who would not have them, at all. Their *"eji ndu eme gini?"* (What is the use of life without honour?) disposed them to suicide. What motivated a white author to describe the Igbo as, "a people before whom the white man feels inferiority complex"? Why do the Yoruba describe Igbo as people who swallow stones without water? Why do the Igbo cause envy and resentment among other Nigerians?

The method of progressivism, which suggests putting oneself in the other person's position, in order to understand and appreciate the other peoples' attitude to us, becomes handy here. Imagine that some 'strange' person comes, apparently empty handed, from an unknown village, very distant from yours. The stranger starts with carrying your 'night soil' or doing other mean jobs. Later he sets up a kiosk, where he sells some 'articles'. The stranger goes on to, over not too long a period, develop a viable big business, and proceeds to build a mansion in that your village, where you have only a hut. He forms the habit of sitting in front of his mansion, in the evenings, exuding more confidence than even the original owners of the land – than yourself!

If the story ends there, what would be your attitude to that erstwhile stranger? Yet, this stranger leaves you with your culture and tradition, including your religion. He installs his practices in your village, among his people and makes no effort to introduce you to his ways, even though he opens if you knock. He takes off to his village, at some of his home festival periods. What would be your attitude to this person? What, if he adds some bad mouth to the situation, always insensitively boasting about his successes. Reader, be honest! Yes, you would start with shocked admiration. Some tinges of envy and jealousy may creep in overtime, and these may mature into resentment and even, open violence! Do the above appear familiar? For the Igbo, it is time to make friends of our host communities! Time to, seriously, endear ourselves to the other Nigerians!

The book, "Ten Reasons Igbo People Are Rich & Successful Business People" lets out "The Secret of Igbo Economic Power". Without saying so, the book reveals the bases of the problems of *Nd'Igbo* in Nigeria and in other countries. The Jews understand this story very well – and so do the Berbers.

Igbo egalitarianism with accompanying upward social mobility, which makes parents pray for their children to be greater than they, and makes masters to pray for their apprentices to overtake them in achievements, combined with a number of Igbo cultural traits or attributes, including achievement orientation, fast acculturation, persistence –the never say die attitude – aggressive application of hard work, competitiveness and confidence etc., make the Igbo hugely successful anywhere they go. And their huge successes left unmanaged, breeds resentment towards them. It is time to device or design ways to manage our success in ways that will endear us to our host communities. It is time to make friends of other Nigerians.

Nigeria has not gained like she should from Igbo successes, in spite of such successes being showcased in every nook and cranny of the country. One reason is that other Nigerians are developing the habit of looking down on the Igbo rather than emulating them. This is because, especially after the civil war, the Igbo are seen as a people excluded from political power. Of the ethnic tripods, on which the country stands, only the Igbo have not supplied an elected Chief Executive Officer of the country. Again, of the six geo-political zones of the country, only the Southeast, home of most Igbo, has not supplied a President of Nigeria. The corruption that is fueled by Oil Money, combined with apparent death of conscience in Nigeria, has weakened values, especially the value of hard work. And so Nigeria grows backwards, remaining in the kindergarten, while those that started the development race with her, are far into the tertiary levels. It seems to be the case that as the Igbo remains down politically, so must Nigeria remain down economically. And this is a lesson, easily deducible from, but not advertised in Humphrey Kanayo Akaolisa's book, which every literate Nigerian should take as a must-read!!!

Okwadike Chukwuemeka Ezeife, CON
                      Ph.D. Harvard (Econs)
Garkuwan Fika, Akintolugboye of Egbaland

PREFACE

WHAT MAKES THE IGBO MAN WHAT HE IS?

In this book Ten Reasons Igbo People are Rich and Successful Business People which gives 'The Secrets of Igbo Economic Power', Humphrey has successfully produced in a very concise book, answers to the enigma – what makes the Igbo man what he is in Nigeria today – admired as he is feared, loved as he is hated, welcome as he is avoided.

A people that are surrounded on all sides by war faring neighbours well organized to face external enemies, yet they are not given to organizing themselves to fight any battle, rather they are comfortable remaining in little groups of autonomous and independent villages governed by council of elders presided by a non-titular head.

A people given to pragmatism, individualism, competitive opportunism and total acceptance of ideology of advancement on the basis of share hard work and merit. They are ready to cling on any change that can bring betterment in their lives and that of their families.

Any new change that can improve Igbo man's wellbeing, he will accept with both hands even if it means jettisoning his home culture, tradition or religion. Western religion and education came later to the east than the west but still "The Igbo wiped out their handicap in one fantastic burst of energy in twenty years between 1930 and 1950" and rose to a commanding enviable heights all round.

The Igbo man's quick adaptability to any new situation if only to conquer obstacle towards self-improvement in his livelihood has brought his dispersal to all parts of Nigeria and beyond. His pursuit for a decent life and happiness for him and his family is paramount to any other end in life and he can endure various privations if only to attain it. In seeking gainful employment, he can assimilate his host culture, and language especially if only for him to get what he wants.

Self-help and help of his community members are paramount including transfer of technology through apprenticeship.

In a style of unmatched simplicity and candor, Humphrey has succeeded in presenting a "must read" handbook or ten Commands of Igbo man's advancement.

This book is recommended to all Igbo and non-Igbo people in Nigeria and Diaspora to widen their understanding of what makes an Igbo man what he is.

Chief S. N. Okeke OON (Ochendo)
B.Sc. (LON) FNIVS, FRICS, LLD

PREFACE II

Often, Igbo people are seen as a problem to other Nigerians. They are generally misunderstood because of their attitude. In my thinking, Igbo people are not always what people feel they are. What we need is to try and understand this people for what they truly are. This book, Ten Reasons... has studied the Igbo people and given different perspectives that can help us have a better understanding of them. The Igbo creativity and talents in great and successful business enterprises or business management did not come by chance. It is a good attribute which many of us wise Nigerians should learn from. My best friends are of Igbo origin. Now one can see the reasons behind Igbo prowess in business, not just in trade, but whatever is called serious business.

The contributions of this book is good for the Igbo man who should cherish the understanding of himself. It would help him see a reason to continue to cultivate and advance some of his good social endowments consciously, and to make adjustments where necessary. It is also good for us Nigerians who may want to emulate or learn from this business secret of the Igbo. I recommend it to all Nigerians.

Chief Gabriel Agada KSJ
                Chairman, Chida Int'l Hotel
The Omachi of Attah Igala

AUTHOR'S NOTE

This book is on an aspect of the rich culture of Igbo people of Southern Nigeria. The book serves a dual purpose, as history on one hand and as a deep and intensive study of the Igbo people with the view of helping to understand this people on the other. It is well known in Nigeria that the Igbo man has been greatly misunderstood by other Nigerians. This lack of understanding of the Igbo has led to hatred and great mishaps including the civil war of 1967-1970 in which the rest of Nigeria teamed up against the Igbo.

The civil war might have been a movement towards a balance of power because the Igbo became too powerful in the Nigerian polity. What do you expect when the Igbo had the economy at the base of their ascension to power? It was no surprise therefore how the Igbo could easily rise in intellectual and political power and became imperial in a country that has over 250 ethnic nationalities. The simplest answer is to say that everything was determined by the cultural background that the people came from. The culture of the Igbo though conflicted with European's at colonization was better oriented for growth and easy assimilation of the cultural changes that were imposed on Africa. It was also quicker in reacting to taking advantage of the new system in contrast to the Western Nigeria that had well knitted culture of feudalism and Northern Nigeria that had well established hierarchies.

The Igbo progressed tremendously under the colonial system because the colonial system was fairly impartial and encouraged initiatives by favouring competency and right qualifications. But the birth of a new Nigeria at independence in 1960 marked the beginning of a system where individual progress would no longer depend on the rules set by the colonial umpire. It also marked the period when the paradigm shift from emphasis on economic development to political interests began. It was not long before the Achilles heel of the culture of the Igbo that constituted an impediment to them in the new system became exposed.

It suffices to say that Nigeria, including the Igbo man may have gone the wrong direction by placing politics ahead of economic development in the scale of preference. Perhaps that is why Nigeria has gone so fast down the drain. Each ethnic nationality in Nigeria has her own strong points and weaknesses. It is not by accident that these nationalities of different talents and human resources were brought together. It must be a Divine design.

It would be right if Nigeria could eschew sentiments and try to harness the abundant resources in her disposal. Such potentials like the Igbo high business initiatives are qualities Nigerian anthropologist would have delved deeply into studying and analyzing with the view of exploiting them for the good of Nigeria. It is not by chance that Igbo people produced many economists and mathematicians of World repute and it would be great if Nigeria could develop and export more of these qualities to the world.

This book, ten reasons Igbo people are rich and successful business people really contains very many secrets about the Igbo development and sustenance of significant economic power, not just in Nigeria but all over the world. It makes a deep study of the Igbo people with the view of bringing to focus the distinctive elements that have made the Igbo good and successful business people.

Indeed there are more than ten reasons that gave the Igbo this distinctive quality but in this book, they have been simplified under ten headings. The book offers very great insight into the Igbo business prowess in a way that should interest every Igbo man that would want to understand what he may have been doing ignorantly and to the world that should learn some lessons from it.

It is not easy to articulate and try to compress the rich culture and all the immense factors that have led to the Igbo successes in various endevours under such a simple heading and few pages. I was bent on trying to do this for the very reason of simplification, bearing in mind, according to H. D. Thoreau, that "Our life is frittered away by detail...simplify! Simplify!"

Humphrey Kanayo Akaolisa Obikwelu
Philosopher

INTRODUCTION

THE IGBO PEOPLE OF SOUTH-EASTERN NIGERIA

Igbo is a part of the Negro race of West Africa. As one of the over 250 nations in Nigeria, they are also one of the three main nations in Nigeria. This is because of their population and influence. The traditional home of the Igbo people is the South-Eastern part of Nigeria and they are surrounded by the Igala, Idoma and Tiv in the North, the Delta City States (Urhobo, Ijaw, and Ogoni) in the South, the Edo, Bini in the West and the Efik and Ibibio in the South East. At present, they occupy the five states of Anambra, Imo, Enugu, Abia, Ebonyi, a greater percentage of Delta and Rivers States and parts of Akwa-Ibom and Benue. The impact of slave trade of the 15th to 19th century was that some Igbo slaves were abandoned in Sierra Leone by the slave traders at the abolition of slave trade and they founded some Igbo speaking communities there in the 19th century. There are also Igbo communities in Liberia, Cameroun and Equatorial Guinea.

Other results of the trans-Atlantic slave trade were that Igbo slaves were also dispersed to Barbados in large numbers, Olaudah Equiano, the famous Igbo author, abolitionist and ex-slave, was dropped off on Barbados after being kidnapped from his hometown near the Bight of Biafra. After arriving in Barbados he was promptly shipped to Virginia. *(Olaudah Equiano 1967).*

Ethnic groups were fairly saturated in certain parts of the Americas because of planters' preferences in certain African peoples. The Igbo were dispersed to colonies such as Haiti, Jamaica, Cuba, Hispaniola, Belize, Trinidad and Tobago, Virginia and Maryland, United States of America. Some slaves arriving in Haiti included Igbo people, here they were considered suicidal and therefore were unwanted by plantation owners. The reason Igbo slaves were suicidal may only be traced by understanding the Igbo within the context of their social background. According to Prof. Adiele Afigbo there is still the Creole saying of *Ibos pend'cor'a yo* (the Ibo hang themselves). *(Herskovits M.J. 1964, pg. 21)* Aspects of Haitian culture that exhibit this can be seen in the *Ibo loa*, a Haitian loa (or deity) created by the Igbo in the Vodun religion. *(Lovejoy P. 2000 pg. 58)*

Within the areas, where the Igbo language is spoken in Nigeria, one may also notice a kind of disparity in dialects and cultures. Definitely, every culture has a spatial and definite geographical distribution of traits, complexes and patterns. This attribute of culture introduces the concept of culture area, which is an anthropological one based on the empirical observation at a given period. Onwuejeogwu defines a cultural area as "a geographical delimitation of areas that have the same dominant and significant culture traits, complexes and pattern. A culture area may have culture centers where the highest frequency of the significant culture traits occur as well as culture margins, where these cultures tend to thin out or overlap with culture traits of another neighbouring culture area'. *(Onwuejeogwu 1975, p.1)*

The Igbo culture area is an area delimitable by an imaginary line running outside the settlement of Agbor, Kwale, Obiaruku, Ebu (West Niger Igbo Areas) Ahoada, Diobu, Umuagbayi (Port-Harcourt area) Arochukwu, Afikpo, Ndinioafu, Isiogo (Abakaliki Areas) and Enugu Ezike (Nsukka Area) and Nzam. This imaginary line encloses an area in which the people not only speak the various dialects of the Igbo language but also share typical and significant common culture traits and patterns up to or above 50%. *(Onwuejeogwu M. A. 1975)*

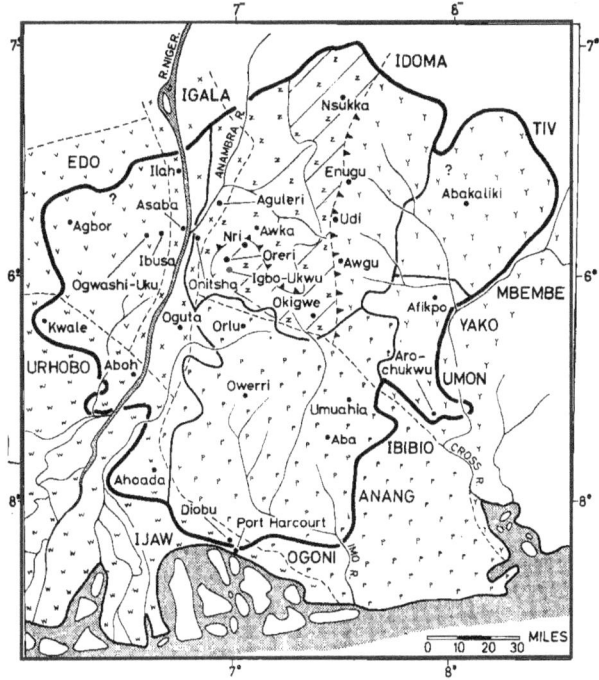

Map of Igbo speaking area, their tribal neighbours and the Cultural divisions.

Apart from these areas that may be designated as the traditional and in some cases adopted home territory of the Igbo people; Igbo people are found in large numbers in every big city of the world and in all the nooks and crannies of Nigeria. They are seen as petty traders, businessmen, business agents, government officials, professionals, doctors, professors and teachers, migrant farmer, company and skill workers, craftsmen, small and big entrepreneurs, transport owners and agents etc.

IGBO INFLUENCE IN NIGERIA

Before the amalgamation of the Nigeria States, the Igbo people fell under the Eastern State colonized by Britain. Prior to the arrival of the colonial masters, within the interior of Africa, there was fragmentation of kingdoms. Apart from the few kingdoms that were brought together by some powerful leaders like the Emperor Menelik II of Ethiopia, Sayyid Said of Zanzibar, Shaka of Zululand and Natals, Moshesh of Bassuto (Lesotho) nations etc., other kingdoms of Africa were fragmented. *(Basil Davidson 1961)*

To the question of this fragmentation, some reasoned that it is because there was abundance of land in Africa and people could therefore migrate and found new kingdoms. Others thought that it was because Africans were more interested in the number of people they were able to rule than in the area of land they acquired. This is unlike the feudal lords of Europe who were interested in the land and property they acquired. This also formed part of the enigmas, which the Europeans had to contend with when they first invaded Igbo land. As Karl Marx observed about the European feudal lords, "In insolent conflict with king and parliament, the great feudal lords created an incomparably larger proletariat by the forcible driving of the peasantry from the land, to which the latter had the same feudal right as the lord himself, and by the usurpation of the common lands." *(Marx K. 1969, pg. 12)*

In contrast to that, "To start with, the British found Igbo land densely populated, but going hand in hand with this dense population was a political situation which baffled and exasperated the average European used to seeing human beings organized in nation states, or at least in the tribal states. The Igbo did not form a state yet by all the rules of the game known to Europeans, they should have formed a state or should have been conquered and incorporated into a state by the one of their neighbours. For one thing, to the West and Northwest, they were flanked by centralized imperialistic and militaristic states, Benin and Idah. It is thought that these states should have partitioned Igbo land or the need for self-defense against Benin and Idah should have compelled the Igbo to come together politically and administratively.

For another thing, the dense population, squeezed as it was within a very small area of land, should have led to fierce wars for land and therefore to state formation, but neither situation had forced the Igbo to organize themselves into a state on the pattern of Benin and Idah. Instead, each little group of villages remained autonomous and independent, governed by a council of elders presided over by some personage occupying the titular position of either *Okpala* or *Isi Ali* or *Obi* or *Eze*." *(Afigbo 1975 p.14)*

It was easy for the Britain to rule a large area in the Northern Nigeria through the Emirs and the same was for the Western Nigeria through the established Obas. The situation was not the same for the Igbo and the similar societies in Eastern Nigeria. Whereas, they could colonize a wide area of an Islamic state by simply signing a treaty with the Emir or defeating his army in a single war and likewise for the Yoruba and the Bini who had well established feudalism, 'the British in Igbo land had to engage town after town and village after village for the simple reason that each of these constituted a city state with an independent government which recognized no exterior masters. As late as 1906, there were parts of Igbo land, which no white man had seen and British control over the subdued areas was anything but secure and complete.' *(Isichei E. 1973, pg. 136)* Some of the established kings of Igbo descent like King Jaja of Opobo fought the British to a stand-still in Southern Nigeria.

It was more or less a cardinal belief of these administrators that every society must have some kind of ruler or a chief and perhaps if there were none at present, because of crisis, that it would be a welcomed gesture to help them achieve such. This is why the British administrators thought it necessary to create structures that would resemble what they found in the north, hence found the warrant chief phenomenon. P.C. Lloyd in Africa in Social Change published in 1972 records the failure of the experiment in indirect rule.

"In attempt to "find a Chief," men were often selected whose traditional roles had little to do with political authority. They were ritual experts or merely presided over councils of elders with equal status. Indeed, the introduction of indirect rule of the Northern Nigeria pattern to the Igbo people and their similarly organized neighbours of Eastern Nigerian proved impossible. From the beginning of the century, administrative officers had created warrant

Chiefs; men who often had no traditional authority but who seemed powerful enough to act as British agents in recruiting labour. Then, when the direct taxation was introduced in 1927, widespread rioting, led by Ibo women, disclosed the extent of hostility to these warrant Chiefs. In 1930s, therefore, councils were instituted which were based upon traditional political units and their representation." *(Lloyd P. C. 1972)*

The difficulties the British encountered in ruling the Igbo people and the other people of Eastern Nigeria was perhaps the reason the British favoured the other parts of the country in the leadership of the nation in the neo-colonial agenda till this date.

The British Colonialists amalgamated Nigeria in 1914. This amalgamation pitched the Igbo people with about 250 other ethnic groups with different languages, cultures and histories in one country. In contrast to the other ethnic groups in this amalgamation who were more politically organized, the Igbo came to Nigeria with their characteristic egalitarianism, individualism, competitiveness, taste for achievement, hard-work and clamorous democracy.

It is important to note here that the Igbo people took advantage of every good thing that came their way. "In many instances, Igbo communities went out of their way to invite missionaries, first to establish mission stations, and then to run schools among them. Often, in addition to providing land, they also had to build the school and pay the teachers from their migre income. To do so, they levied themselves and provided labour" *(Oguejiofor J. 1996 P.26)*. Before the amalgamation of Nigeria, the Igbo people were already far ahead of many other people in the amalgamation with regard to education.

"The Igbo culture being receptive to change, individualistic and highly competitive gave the Igbo man an unquestioned advantage over his compatriots in securing credentials for advancement in Nigeria colonial society. Unlike the Hausa-Fulani, he was unhindered by a wary religion and unlike the Yoruba unhampered by traditional hierarchies. This kind of creature; fearing nor God nor man, was custom-made to grasp the opportunities, such as they were, of the white man's dispensation. And the Igbo did so with both hands." *(Achebe, C. 1989 pg. 58)*

Under the colonial amalgamation, and partly because of the population pressure (squeezed in a small unproportional area), the Igbo came to see all the other parts of the country as a fair field for play and for business. They spread out in large numbers as traders, mission agents, government officials, teachers, migrant farmers and so on. The wider area of operation offered by the Nigerian reality and even beyond gave them the opportunity of putting into advantage personality traits that have sediment in them through the passage of centuries.

It is also important to note that the Igbo did not just move out of their forest home all because of the population pressure. There are largely great areas of the Igbo forest home territories that are still untouched to this day. The Igbo desire for improvement lies largely beneath this proclivity. "Although the Yoruba had a huge historical and geographical head-start, the Igbo wiped out their handicap in one fantastic burst of energy in the twenty years between 1930 and 1950." *(Achebe, C. Op. cit.)*

There is also an unquestionable fact about the Igbo people and their similar south-eastern neighbours being the only groups in the Nigeria entity that fully accepted this amalgamation from the unset and even till today. They travelled to all parts of Nigeria, settled, built permanent structures and were eager to be assimilated as natives of their host communities. They equally learn the language and cultures of their hosts and even take their titles.

"The Igbo therefore left their forest state and scattered far and wide in search of personal improvement in different areas of life. They are found in good numbers in almost every part of Nigeria and beyond. Typically, they arrive with nothing except their determination and their readiness to work. Typically too, they made good within considerable short period of time but in their un-condescending tenacity and their boisterous attitude, they incur the fear, envy, jealousy and sometimes outright hatred and aggression of people among whom they live." *(Oguejiofor J. Loc. cit.)*

The Igbo people were tremendously successful under the colonial regime all over Nigeria. They played a principal role in the winning of Nigeria independence in 1960. People at the fore included Dr. Nnamdi Azikiwe, the first Premier of Eastern Nigeria, the first Nigeria President of the Senate, first Nigerian Governor-General and the first Nigerian President at independence, others include; Dr. K.O. Mbadiwe, M. I. Okpara, Prof. Kenneth Dike, Alvan Ikoku, Akanu

Ibiam, Mbonu Ojike, Sir Loius Mbanefo, Denise Osadebe, Nwafor Orizu who was the Second Nigeria Senate President and first Nigeria Acting President, and a host of other business men including Chief Odumegwu Ojukwu, the first millionaire in Africa and the father of Colonel Chukwuemeka Odumegwu Ojukwu the leader of the Biafra secession. Other people in the military include; General Thomas Aguiyi-Ironsi who became the first Nigeria Military Head of State and Major Chukwuma Nzeogwu who led the first Military Coup-de-tat in Nigeria and perhaps in Africa. Chief Edwin Umeozeoke was the first Speaker of the House of Representatives, while Dr. Alexander Ekwueme was the first Vice President of Nigeria. The role of the Igbo people in Nigeria has been that of pioneering in every quarter.

Chinua Achebe has been renowned as the foremost African writer; with him were Cyprian Ekwensi, Christopher Okigbo, Gabriel Okara and Elechi Amadi. Chief Emeka Anyaoku was the first African Secretary General of the Common-wealth. Professor Chike Obi is the first Nigerian Mathematician and Professor of Mathematics. Cardinal Francis Arinze is the first African to command a significant position in the Vatican and Blessed Iwene Tansi the Venerable will soon be declared the first Nigerian Catholic Saint. In science, Philip Emeagwali has the international recognition as inventing the world fastest computer, and winner of 1989 Gordon Bell Prize, while Professor Bart. Nnaji is renowned as a world expert in Robotics.

In sports, Emmanuel Ifeajuna was the first sports man to write the name of Nigeria in world sports history when he became the first African sportsman to win a gold medal at a global sports event, namely the Commonwealth Games of Vancouver Canada in 1954. A new Commonwealth record for the high jump was established at the games by Emmanuel Ifeajuna of Nigeria, who became the first Commonwealth athlete to clear six feet and nine inches. Dick Tiger Ihetu and Power Mike Okpara in the 60s won Nigeria's first World belts in boxing and wrestling respectively. Chioma Ajunwa won the first Nigeria Olympic Gold Medal while Kanu Nwankwo and John Mikel Obi are two of the only three Nigerians that have won the European Champions league. Kanu led Nigeria to the first African Olympic Gold medal in football. Christian Chukwu and Stephen Okechukwu Keshi had led Nigeria in 1980 and 1994 respectively to winning the African Cup of Nations the only two occasions Nigeria had won it. This is just to mention a few of the Igbo people influence in Nigeria and achievement world over.

Consequently the Igbo for their successes in wherever they are found became the victims of communal riots and threats of them wherever they went in Nigeria. Nzeogwu, a devout Igbo son but a detribalized Nigerian, planned a nationalist coup that was foiled by another Igbo man, General Aguiyi Ironsi, after some Northern chieftains have been murdered in cold-blood. "A misunderstanding of the motives behind the January (1966) coup led to the Northern revenge or rather 'over-revenge' as witnessed by the May riots, the July counter-coup and the massacres of September-October 1966. A similar misunderstanding of the intentions behind the actions of the Federal Government after these massacres led many

Easterners, especially Ibos, to believe that what has happened was a planned attempt to exterminate them." *(Uwechue R. 1971, pg. 32)*

Writers and other social publicists started drawing parallels between the Igbo people of Nigeria and the Jews around Europe and the world for this reason *(Afigbo A. E. 1975)*. On the one hand are the Igbo business acumen and their suffering at the hands of other Nigerian ethnic nationalities and on the other hand is the Jewish experience throughout history. The targeting of Igbo people at political and religious violence in and around Nigeria, have most times been likened to the *"Jewish Holocaust"* of the World War II.

Other factors that have led to people drawing these parallels include some religious and cultural similarities that could be found in the two cultures; such traits as circumcision, the system and manner of naming children, sentence structure and similarities in word sounds, dual organization, ritual symbolisms, a supreme God and religion in general. *(Akaolisa H. K. 2003 pg. 156)*

The other important point is the embattled Biafra between 1967 and 1970 when the rest of Nigeria teamed against the Igbo people in a war that presented a near perfect parallel to the state of Israel surrounded by hostile Arab Nations who occasionally team up against them. The Igbo did not only make this comparison but believed in it. They also came to hope that they would weather the Nigeria storm just as the Israeli are weathering the Arab storm. Thus, there are many enlightened Igbo of the post Biafra war whom the claim on eastern origin is neither mere history nor the *'Oriental mirage'* of Salomon Reinach but an ideology for group survival. *(Afigbo 1975)* The extent this claim can be sustained is yet an open question and is not of any concern to this work.

One confusing aspect of the war was that Major Nzeogwu, the originator of the crises is of Western Igbo origin, a part of Igbo land that falls within the Mid-western region of Nigeria in the colonial boundaries. But the seceding State of Biafra was primary made up by the Eastern Region which was only predominantly Igbo. There was no plan on irredentism on the part of Igbo against colonial boundaries or on integration of the non-Igbo within the so called *Biafra State*. It goes to prove that the war was just a mere expression of ethnic sentiments against the Igbo and the Igbo acting in self-defend. There was no prior plan to form a State or wage a war. The result was a manifestation of the Igbo suicidal inclination in fighting a course.

Post war Nigeria had policies that aimed specifically at cutting down on the powers and influence of Igbo people in Nigeria. For instance, "Chief Obafemi Awolowo, Federal Commissioner for Finance, under his guidance a banking policy was evolved which nullified any bank account which had been operated during the civil war. This had the immediate result of pauperizing the Igbo middle class and earning a profit of £4 million for the Federal Government Treasury. The *'Indigenization Decree'* which followed soon afterwards completed the routing of Igbo from commanding heights of Nigerian economy, to everyone's apparent satisfaction." *(Achebe, C. 1989)* The indigenization was executed just after the war, a time when no Igbo man had enough capital to buy into any of the companies that were indigenized.

The policy of indigenization marked the end to the era of competitive and productive economic progress in Nigeria. The collapse was also accelerated by the policy of *'Centralization of the Economy'* depriving the different Regions and later States the power of self-productive determination. It also master-minded the acceleration of the institutionalization of corruption and mediocrity. Productive initiative was there and then stagnated. States and Local Governments up till today have to sit and wait monthly for Federal allocations, while people continually call for more and more States and Local Governments creation to ensure more allocations. *'Federal Character'* or *'Quota System'* also came in vogue and permeated every sector including sports. All these policies were put in place in a bid to put the Igbo man's advancement in a cage.

There were also conscious efforts to deny the Igbo people access to basic amenities such as good roads, power and electricity, quality schools etc. To control the Igbo advancement, the Government took over all private owned schools. Igbo people from their inclination to hard work and industry were already at the time developing indigenous manufacture in Aba, Onitsha, Awka, Nnewi etc. But after the war, Igbo products of industry were thence designated with derogatory terms like *'Igbo-made', 'Aba-made', 'Onitsha-made'* etc. which then instituted across the Country a general contempt for made in Nigeria products. And thus began the decline in Nigeria indigenous manufacture and general preference for foreign products made in Taiwan, made in China, made in Japan, made in Hong-Kong etc. The international force on liberalization of economies presented a good landing for the Nigerian Government to throw its boarder open to foreign goods rather than see the indigenous manufacture led by Igbo people see the light of day.

Other impact was that of different kinds of schism rising among the Igbo. Though such schismatic tendencies existed prior to the war or within the Igbo system, it was tremendously coloured by the civil war. After the war, an Igbo identity was deemed, in many ways, a disadvantage. As a result, many Igbo communities, especially in the present Rivers and Delta States would vigorously deny being Igbo, yet in all intensity, they bear every Igbo culture ranging from the language to the least of all the traits. Prof. B. Nwabueze observed, "Some of the Igbo border communities in Bendel (now Delta) State as well as those in and around Port-Harcourt now strenuously disclaim their Igbo identity. The disclaimer is manifested in practical terms by the latter changing the name of their villages by prefixing them with an 'R' so that Umuokoro becomes Rumokoro, Umuigbo becomes Rumuigbo... The intension is to make them not look or sound Igbo names" *(Nwabueze, 1985 p.4)*

In Delta State, we find the alteration of certain names like Igbo-Uzo (literary meaning "on the way Igbo") being styled to Ibuzo or Ibusa. Most of the people in this area would ridiculously accept that they belong to the culture "Ibo" and not "Igbo" whereas the term 'Ibo' is well known to have originated from the aberrations set on the term Igbo by the Europeans who could not pronounce the alphabet 'gb'. More ridiculously, this same people in the spoken language by typical indigenes would use "Igbo" as the term but only to be found in written form as "Ibo" perhaps perpetrated by the learned few. *(Akaolisa 2003)*

In spite of the moves to pauperize the Igbo people after the war they have returned very quickly to take back the control of almost the entire micro economy of Nigeria and parts of the bureaucratic institutions. In spite of the marginalization from government and institution of economic policies by subsequent governments that aim to crush out or check-mate the growth of the Igbo economic power, they have remained a force to be reckoned with. They may not have been part of the looting of the National treasury but a substantial wealth from people who loot the country somehow finds its way into the hands of the Igbo. Their build up in business is gradual and purposeful. In the imagery of J. P. Clark, they are like the *"ants filing out of the wood"* moving out of their forest home, they have scattered and seized the floor.

The State of Biafra may be said to have failed, but the Igbo as a people has not. This is because the policy of marginalization had other positive effects on the Igbo people; that of hardening the people all the more. The Igbo people came back to Nigeria with more determination to seek equity within the Nigerian state. In spite of the difficulties so far encountered, the Igbo in their usual tenacity and positivity have not given up and may never do so unless Nigeria takes the other option of disintegrating or allowing Biafra to secede. This may continue to be a possibility if the rest of Nigeria continues to fail to see and appreciate the Igbo as *'The Salt of Nigeria'*.

There were some perceptible drop in education in the 70s because of the marginalization of the Igbo in Nigeria. A lot of Igbo people in the high government profile jobs lost their appointments after the war. Many then felt more secured with the businesses they could control both the capital and location. The few Igbo people that still considered investments on education insisted on professional courses. The result was that Nigeria began making some significant loss in talents. At the same time the challenge was good for the Igbo people who now concentrated on higher and professional education to make them less dependent on the Nigeria system and seeking lucrative employments abroad.

In this vein, with increasing knowledge about the world and increased globalization, the Igbo people saw the opportunity to widen the horizon of migration to other parts of Africa and the entire world. And thus began also a massive brain-drain of the best Igbo product of industry that now migrated abroad to work in the United kingdom, United States and other parts of Europe and the world. From the streets of Pretoria and Johannesburg to Tripoli, Dakar and Maputo, Igbo people are the Nigerians that today dominate the Businesses in African cities. From Rio to Oklahoma, from Shanghai to Hamburg and from Osaka to London, Igbo people are found in all works of life and with tremendous successes.

Prominent Igbo communities outside Africa include those of London in the United Kingdom and Houston, California, Atlanta, and Washington, D.C. in the United States. With genealogy tracing by means of DNA testing, the roots of the African diaspora is being uncovered by descendants of the victims of the Atlantic slave trade who are researching their family history. In the 2003 PBS program *African American Lives*, Bishop T.D. Jakes had his DNA analyzed; his Y chromosome showed that he is descended from the Igbo. American actors Forest Whitaker, Paul Robeson, and Blair Underwood have traced their genealogy back to the Igbo people. *(Wikipedia Retrieved 2.12.2012)*

"The Igbo are very numerous. There is educated guess that if Nigeria's census is properly enumerated, the Igbo could easily be the largest ethnic group in the country. They may number up to 40 million. Everything right now, is speculation. Nobody knows the true stratification or ethnic populations in Nigeria. The Igbo are the only ethnic group found in large numbers everywhere in Nigeria, and foreign countries more than any other ethnic group in Africa."*(Uju Nkwocha Afulezi 2010 article)*

To support this view, Oxford African Encyclopedia for Schools and Colleges of 1974 described the home territory of the Igbo people as "where the density of population is highest in West Africa." *(Oxford African Encyclopedia, 1974 pg. 260)* Migrations from this part of Nigeria to other parts were in fact reduced drastically from the years after the war than it had been before it. So Igbo people migration cannot account for the sudden change in the distribution of populations within Nigeria after the war nor could the war account for that.

Uju's guess is also supported by the fact that it is ridiculous to continue to believe that in the whole of the Sub-Saharan Coast of West African, when moving from the Atlantic Ocean to the Sahara in the North, the population is decreasing is not obtainable in Nigeria. This is contrary to nature. From Guinea Bissau to Senegal, Ivory Coast, Ghana, Mali, Togo, from Benin Republic in the West of Nigeria to the Cameroun in the East and Niger in the North, all obey this natural order. It is only in Nigeria that the reverse is the case; this is only possible because here is Nigeria, the only place in the world it is possible that the Sea flows to the River, where *'it is written Manchester but pronounced Liverpool'*. This is the social environment and system that the Igbo people have found themselves in the modern Nigeria.

The reason for which the Igbo people are very business minded and successful business people cannot be removed from the social, political and economic environment/development of this people. The harsh and changing social and political environment that the Igbo people find themselves is on one hand an impetus for their development. The social norms, traditional beliefs and world views are on the other. It is partly on this basis that I have meditated and tried to articulate this little work.

In the work, I have not aimed at making any apologia for the Igbo people so that anyone should read this book with open mind.

1
IGBO WORLDVIEW, ADAPTABILITY TO CHANGE AND CULTURES ASSIMILATION

In Ejiofor's study of the *Umuezechima* kingdoms of Igbo land, he noted that "a focal point for understanding individual and group behaviour of the people of *Umuezechima* is the value which they place on the 'good life'. Good life, as used here, is not a moral expression; rather, it describes a life which surpasses sheer subsistence. Man does not only exist in order to scratch hard for his sustenance; he identifies his life interests in abundance, free movement, good feeding and happy social life. Short of Epicureanism, the search for happiness is for him an end which validates and justifies any means that facilitates that search." *(Ejiofor L. 1982 pg. 38)*

The focal point of search in the Igbo worldview explains the reason why the Igbo is ready to make any adjustment or change that will ultimately lead him to this quest. However, the means that is overtly appreciated by the society is the genuine means.

The Igbo culture is therefore distinct by its readiness and ability to accept changes. One may rightly say that partly, the socio-political structure and the worldview of the Igbo people formed the bases for their receptivity to change. The Igbo generally show a deep sense of pragmatism. There are really very few absolutes in Igbo traditions.

"The Igbo sometimes possess unbelievable ability to endure hardship. This hardship must, in some manner, be perceived as the best option under the given circumstances. This means that if a better alternative is seen, they will readily abandon their former option for the latter one". *(Oguejiofor J. 1996 pg.25)* The Igbo do not believe in any kind of determinism or pre-destination. Much depends on your hard work and ability to advance oneself. In *"Things Fall Apart"* despite the destiny of Unoka, Okonkwo's father, Okonkwo believed that he could change his future through hard work. *(Achebe C. 1985)*

It is one of the most ingrained beliefs among the Igbo that no condition is permanent. This is greatly demonstrated in the extreme social mobility of their communities. *(B. Davidson, 1969. pg. 95).* In the book title *The Igbo Race, Origin and Controversies*, Akaolisa x-rayed the different schisms in Igbo history and reasons and patterns of Igbo dispersals, bifurcations, migrations, confluences, fusions and incorporations. *(Akaolisa, 2003 pg. 21)* In 1938, Basden wrote of the Igbo that "Their readiness to travel and their tenacity of purpose, especially when seeking gainful employment, have carried many of them far beyond their native environment. When abroad, they maintain close contact, cemented and sustained by a strong tribal bond of union. Whatever the conditions, the Ibo immigrants adapt themselves to meet them, and it is not long before they make their presence felt in the localities where they settle." *(Basden, 1966 pg. xi)*

The Igbo concept of God and the supernatural, and their attitude towards the innumerable divinities is at the basis of all these traits. Belief in the supernatural also shaped the socio-cultural and personality traits which have sediment among the Igbo people. Their conception of the supernatural has made it possible for them to adapt to any circumstance, because the Igbo have a kind of pragmatic relations with their divinities in which they have their destiny in their own hands and not in the hand of the divinities; a kind of an anthropocentric worldview.

"Igbo relationship with their divinities has been aptly described as a reciprocal or contractual relation in which each party is expected to fulfill his own part of the contract". *(Nze C. 1981 pg. 23)* The divinities are cultivated. They are fed with both seasonal and occasional sacrifices. Those that are public have shrines erected in their honour, and priests who attend to their needs. They usually have their taboos which are very strictly observed. But having done these, the Igbo expect their divinities to protect them, enrich them, or at least take charge of the particular sphere for which each is cultivated. It is not uncommon that the divinities fail in their duties. When they do so, the Igbo feel no qualms in inviting sanctions on them. *(Oguejiofor op. cit. pg. 76)*

One typical example of this behaviour in the Igbo people is the scenario painted by Achebe in *Arrow of God,* with the fracas that developed between Ezeulu, the chief priest of Ulu, and Nwaka the rich and popular orator. In one of the most popular scenes, Nwaka denied the Chief Priest of the gods in charge of collective security, the right to determine war policy. Ezeulu has just summed up their opposing attitude towards the divine in the war debate when he announced, " No matter how strong or great a man was, he should never challenge his *'Chi'* in a proverb that designated Nwaka as the little bird *'Nza'* that when it had eaten to its satisfaction, challenge his god to a wrestling combat *"Nwa nza rijuolu afo, chee chi ya aka mgba".* To this we have seen Nwaka reply with another proverb thus; "If a man says yes, his *'Chi'* also says yes" *"Onye kwe, chi ya ekwe".* One was saying that man must be subordinate and subservient to the divine while the other insists that the divine is an expression or an agent of the human, which now raised a more fundamental problem of the nature of divinity in the Igbo world view. Nwaka, as warning or a threat to Ezeulu on the possibility of the people abandoning him and his god, cited the example of a similar event in another village to demonstrate that Ulu the deity could not take the people of Umuaro to ransom for no just cause. *(Achebe C. 1981 pg.134)*

Ultimately it discloses the nature of Igbo adaptability to any circumstance. There is always a matching opposing ideology to any one ideology that is hegemonic; a standard that leaves a window or a door open to continue in another direction without any crippling absolute. This is not found only with the divinities but also in every other aspect of the Igbo life. For instance, it is said that: '*Onye ndidi na eri azu ukpo.*' literally meaning that the patient man eats the fattest fish. While on the other hand somebody may equally contend that: '*Anu bu uzo na anu mmiri oma*', literally meaning that the first animal to get to the stream always enjoys the fresh or clean water. Both statements are opposing extremes that create a strong ground for one to continue rightfully on either.

This perception of the world and divinity has cultivated in the Igbo man ingrained dynamism, progressiveness and their receptivity to change. Igbo receptivity to change, which testifies to their pragmatism and adaptability, has also generated some interpretations on the Igbo people. The British anthropologist Leith-Ross portrayed the Igbo as a people who have no sense of history, and whom, as a result, the future was the only dimension of time that is important. 'The young men,' she declares, 'are content to have no past so long as they have a future.' *(Leith-Ross op. cit. pg. 54)* According to Oguejiofor, 'given the Igbo person's attachment to his community (origin), such an unnuanced statement is surprising. We can nevertheless glean from it the undeniable fact that the Igbo are very forward-looking. Tradition (the past) is indeed very important, but the Igbo refuse to make it a crippling absolute. Such an attitude has had a tremendous impact on the people, their culture, and their religion.'

A remarkable case in point is Igbo reception of western education and subsequently Christianity. The first missionaries arrived in Igbo land in the second half of the 19th century. They were received peacefully. The missionaries found the Igbo people very rich and proud people. Missionary work did not attract much following, and the first converts were mostly descendants of recaptives or slaves bought over by missionaries and the out-lawed *(osu)* who formed the foundation of Christian villages (established by the Catholic missionaries). Efforts to lure the majority Igbo people to the Church through offering them gifts did not make any impression on them. Rather through a combination of factor, including the works of charity like healing sick people and the evident stance of some of the missionaries against the brutalities perpetrated against the Igbo by British trading companies, the missionaries came with time to acquire a good reputation among the Igbo.

Nevertheless, it was not until the missionaries began the work of education, something that certainly promised a better future for the Igbo, that they witnessed an almost unbelievable explosion of converts to their message. In many instance, Igbo communities went out of their way to invite missionaries, first to establish mission stations, and then to run schools among them. Often, in addition to providing land, they also had to build the schools and pay the teacher from their little income. To do so they levied themselves and provided labour. Many of these people did not themselves become educated. They sent their children to school with all the support they needed. These children, in turn, through schooling, accepted to be Christians, and thus began the story of one of the most phenomenal successes of missionary endeavour in the history of Christianity in its entirety. *(Oguejiofor, J. op. cit.)*

The extent this *'phenomenal successes'* of the missionary in the history of the Christendom was achieved is still a big question in some views, considering the behaviour of the African Christian. The Igbo man for example has taken to Christianity his pragmatic relationship with the divinities and this has accounted for the sudden proliferation of the Christian Religion that was brought to him in fewer than three denominations. In the Igbo man quest for success, he would not mind making a change, or trying another Christian denomination that seems to have the answers that he seeks. In many cases, one witnesses the situation where Christianity and the traditional religion and practices co-habit in the same faithful.

Otternberg wrote that the Igbo resented the colonization by Europeans but instead of fighting them, the Igbo tried to acquire their power by education. A movement that was literarily expressed by Achebe in *'Arrow of God'* when Ezeulu in spite of being the chief priest of the highest deity in his community sent his son, Oduche, to school to learn the secret of the white man. It is speculated that as early as the late 19 century, the Igbo people were insightful enough to realize that opportunities would be rosy in the future if they acquire western education. That was the primary concern of the Igbo and not any fascination in the mystery of the incarnation in the white man's religion.

"At first Oduche did not want to go to church. But Ezeulu called him to his obi and spoke to him as a man would speak to his best friend and the boy went forth with pride in his heart. He had never heard his father speak to anyone as an equal.

'The world is changing,' he had told him. 'I do not like it. But I am like the bird *Eneke-nti-oba*. When his friends asked him why he was always on the wing he replied: "Men of today have learnt to shoot without missing and so I have learnt to fly with-out perching." I want one of my sons to join these people and be my eye there. If there is nothing in it you will come back. But if there is something there you will bring home my share. The world is like a Mask dancing. If you want to see it well you do not stand in one place. My spirit tells me that those who do not befriend the white man today will be saying had we known tomorrow'" *(Achebe C. 1977 pg. 46)*

The missionary were ready to provide this education both for their own specific evangelic objectives and the betterment of the people. The Igbo found no hindrance in following these missionaries, accepting their message and also not forgetting to utilize the opportunities which this acceptance brought to them. In accepting Christianity and education, they were not merely fawning on the missionaries. They also had a high price to assure the education of their children. "A parent would starve and deny himself all comforts in life in other to send his child to school; his ambition was to make good in his child what he himself lacked. He might be a peasant farmer, a poor illiterate carpenter or blacksmith, but his dream was to live to see his son become a clerk or even a lawyer, doctor or engineer." *(Nwabueze op. cit. pg. 6)*

Even at that, education did not quite come to them on a Plata of gold. As Walter Rodney rightly observed, "the missionaries asked for the control of schools because that was one of their drawing cards for the church itself and because they considered themselves as experts on the side of cultural imperialism (which they called civilization). However, there were other Europeans both within and without the colonies who were absolutely opposed to schools –be they Christian, Independent, Government or Islamic. Starting from a racist position, they asserted that offering education to Africans was like throwing pearls before swine." *(Rodney W. 1972 pg.300)*

"The same inclination which led the Igbo people to see the value of education many years ago, for which they worked so hard, and were ready to abandon an important aspect of their tradition still remains with them. If they were ready many years ago to defy all odds and to send their children to school, to let them become Christians, abandoning their traditional religion, they are even more ready to do similar things today. Some Igbo intellectuals have recently derided this tendency. Odumegwu-Ojukwu, almost in a tirade, traced how the Igbo, shocked by the impact of colonialism, jettisoned their gods, and embraced new ones in the form of materialism and fawning on the rich. It must be borne in mind in all circumstances that Igbo readiness to do certain things is owed to some underlying traits which can be channeled to laudable and sometimes despicable goals." *(Oguejiofor J. 1996)*

Achebe in a similar vein as Ojukwu wrote off the attitude of the Igbo to leadership and politics, "The bankrupt state of Igbo leadership is best illustrated in the alacrity with which they have jettisoned their traditional republicanism in favour of mushroom kingships. From having no kings in their recent past the Igbo swung round to set an all-time record of four hundred "kings" in Imo and four hundred in Anambra! And most of them are traders in their stall by day and monarchs at night; city dwellers five days a week and traditional village rulers on Saturdays and Sundays! They adopt "traditional" robes from every land, including, I am told, the ceremonial regalia of the Lord Mayor of London." *(Achebe, C. op. cit.)*

Achebe's disgust here on the behaviour of his people should not be taken with great seriousness. Cultures assimilation has been of great advantage to the Igbo progresses world over. The resilience of Igbo culture has been an enduring tool which the Igbo man has used to permeate and outwit their competitors in the Nigerian entity. The Igbo quickly learn the language and culture of his hosts and even that of his guests and put them into positive use immediately. Many Igbo thinkers have hinted on the danger of the Igbo cultures and language going extinct because of this but no event has proved this fear to be tenable. This is because the Igbo community consciousness and depth of culture has no match with that of any of his competitors in Nigeria. The Igbo culture has survived till date in Haiti, Sierra-Leone and in many colonies where Igbo slaves were dumped. The colonial forces and Christianity may have improved and changed the Igbo man to some extent but his quiddity has remained untouched.

Thus as Ottenberg explains, "Yet, paradoxically, of all Nigerian peoples, the Ibo have probably changed the least while changing the most. While many of the formal elements of the social, religious, economic, and political structures, such as lineages, family groups, age grades, and secret societies, have been modified through cultural contact, many of the basic patterns of social behaviour, such as the emphasis on alternative choices and goals, achievement and competition, and the lack of strong autocratic authority have survived and are part of the newly developing culture." *(Ottenberg, S.1959 pg. 130)*

There may never come a time in the future when the place of *'Igbo kwenu'* will be totally taken over by *'Otito dili Jesu'* or when the response *'Ise'* will be totally delete or taken over by *'Amen.'* no matter how much this people are Christianized.

Let me correct some views my postulation on the proliferation of Christian Religion in Igbo land may have provoked. The Igbo man has taken to Christianity his pragmatic relations with the divinities but he has maintained the deep reverence and fear of God or the gods as the case might be. For his fear of God he is not inclined to founding new religions and converting religion into source of material wealth or money making venture as many of the people of western Nigeria do. He may jump from one religion to another but just because of one problem in another sphere of life that he seeks some spiritual resolution. His attitude of making such changes or combining his Christianity with the traditional religion is in resonance with his pragmatic view to life; seeking the solution that works in his quest for success, power and the good life.

Cultism, ritual killings for wealth, secret societies and all sorts of crimes are all parts of the assimilated cultures in Igbo land and not in the indigenous culture of Igbo people. Rarely do you find the head-quarters of any of these Religions sited in Igbo land. The Igbo believe in success through hard work and treat with scorn wealth made by dubious means. Igbo people have quickly assimilated these cultures because of their ambitiousness and pressure from the society that mandates success on them. The repercussions on Igbo who joined such religions are quicker because of the norms (*omenani*) in Igbo land.

Yet the aspect of killing or spilling of human blood has been tasking for Igbo to assimilate. Anambra State for instance is a good example. As the cradle of Igbo culture, the State has been un-arguably the most politically contentious State in Nigeria with most of the big heads. But in spite of the stiff contentions, hardly does one hear of any political killings as we often hear from other States of Nigeria. This is because of the Igbo man's deep respect for human life. Okonkwo in *Things Fall Apart* had to live with the shock of Ikemefuna having to die by his sword for the rest of his life, in spite of his villainy and his doing that in obedience to the command of the gods.

2
ANCIENT TRADING AND DEVELOPMENT OF MERCANTILE

We may never know for certain how trade and marketing developed in ancient Igbo culture. Dr. U. I. Ukwu has expressed the view that they probably developed out of the institution of the Igbo rest day *(Hodder and Ukwu, 1969, p. 126-159).*

Works by Professor Afigbo has shown that Igbo people originally settled on the Northern Igbo plateau; 'most other Igbo groups claim that their ancestors lived on the Northern Igbo plateau before moving out in search of un-occupied land.' *(Afigbo 1975 pg. 37)* This Northern Igbo plateau as matter of clarification is the area of the Igbo land that stretches from Nsukka to Awka to Orlu with Igbo-Ukwu at the peak and center of it. Of all parts of Igbo land, the Northern Igbo area has lost its vegetal cover most. This would suggest that it has been under continuous Igbo occupation for longer than the other parts and the population pressure that led to its loss of its vegetal cover would have led to the development of trade in this area.

Umuezechima for instance, according to Ejiofor are not great traders probably because their agricultural economy is self-supporting and people come from all parts of Nigeria to buy from them. One may note that the big traders among the Igbo come from areas where land is either insufficient or relatively fertile. the Igbo traders east of the Niger are mainly found around Aguata, Awka, Nnewi, Idemili, Arochukwu, Mbaise and Orlu zones where there are high concentrations of population and vast stretches of unarable land. *(Ejiofor L. op. cit. pg. 32)*

Meek observed the character of the Isu as longdistant traders and remarked that "Among men the propensity towards trade varies considerably in different groups. Thus, in Owerri Division, the large groups of people known as the Isu are noted traders, and on any of the main roads leading to Port-Harcourt hundreds of Isu can be seen making their way on foot or on bicycle to and from this center of trade. *(Meek, C. K. 1937)*

In the Northern Igbo tradition, there are mythologies that trade developed in this region in early times. The traditions are definite that trade, markets and marketing were institutionalized by the Igbo high god, *Chukwu*, He sent four heavenly fishmongers who gave their names – *Eke, Orie, Afo,* and *Nkwo* to the Igbo four-day week, established markets and sold fish. *(Afigbo 1975 pg. 44)* This mythology is true to an extent. A deeper study shows that the Northern Igbo area lacks rivers and ponds from which fish could be caught. Thus from earliest times, fish constituted a delicacy among the people as it could only be got from the Niger or Anambra Rivers to the west, or from Cross River to the east, or worse still because of the distance, from Ijaw or the Delta region. The Northern Igbo legends regarding the origin of markets would thus seem to emphasize the point, that trade in Igbo culture originated from the exchange of surplus goods for goods in short supply.

This point is further emphasizes in another legend regarding the origin of cultivated crops. According to the story, after *Nri* had obtained yams, cocoyam, oil palm tree and breadfruit tree from *Chukwu*, the neighbouring peoples brought him livestock and other forms of wealth in exchange for food crops. This in other words was trade by barter. *(Afigbo 1975 pg. 44)* It also buttresses the fact that the first Igbo people that settled in the Northern Igbo plateau were originally livestock farmers before the advent of *Nri* culture who brought some crops.

There are deductions to be drawn from ecological data to support this theory. The Northern Igbo area was the first to be occupied by the Igbo and to be heavily exploited by them. One result of this was that the vegetation soon disappeared while the quality of the soil deteriorated. In this situation, agriculture ceased to be very profitable, in the sense of meeting all the food needs of the Northern Igbo. The people responded to this worsening situation by taking to other professions such as trade, smiting, medicine, the running of oracles and so on. In other words, they developed specialized arts which they peddled among the other Igbo cultural groups whose soils could still support profitable agriculture. In this regard, it is noteworthy that most of the famed traders and other specialists of Igbo land, such as the Awka, Aro,

Nkwelle, Abiriba, Nri, Umudioka and so on are located on the Northern Igbo Plateau and its south-easterly extension through Bende to Arochukwu. *(Afigbo, 1972 pg. 45)*

This is precisely that part of Igbo land where agriculture started failing early in the people's history. Thus regional trade in Igbo land developed, in part, out of the growing ecological differentiation between the Northern Igbo area and the plains and uplands surrounding it.

Another factor was the differential distribution of essential mineral deposits in Igbo land. The Northern Igbo Plateau and its extension to Bende are rich in iron ore deposits. And it was here that smelting and iron-working were most highly developed and practices in Igbo land. The iron tools and implements produced on the plateau were in great demand over the rest of Igbo land and even beyond. On the other hand, in the Northern Igbo area, there are brine springs and lead deposits which would appear to have been exploited from very early times. *(Talbot, 1926)*

The analyses of the coppery objects from Igbo-Ukwu were interestingly found that the majority were of a heavily leaded bronze, containing up to 12% of tin and up to 16% of lead, copper making up the rest. Some other objects were pure copper. The effort by Thurstan Shaw to find the provenance of the materials used in the Igbo-Ukwu bronze showed that there was no exploitable quantity of copper in Nigeria particularly in ancient times. This was based on present reports. According to him, "the nearest source of copper is to the north of Nigeria in the region of the Republic of Niger. Ancient exploitation of copper is known near Akjoujk in Mauritania and around Nioro in the Republic of Mali. There is copper in Dar Fur in the western part of the Republic of Sudan and also in the Katanga and Zambia copper belt, but that is further away. Plentiful sources of tin are available within Nigeria, on and around Jos Plateau and it is known that the inhabitants before the advent of Europeans anciently exploited it. Unfortunately, we do not know how back this exploitation goes. There are lead and zinc deposits in South-Eastern Nigeria, which also show signs of pre-European exploitation. *(Thurstan Shaw, 1977 pg. 45)*

There would appear to have been a demand for lead among the smiths of the Northern Igbo area, *(Onwuejeogwu, 1972 pg. 15-56)*, while salt was in demand throughout Igbo land. Though Igbo needs for salt could not have been met entirely from the North-Eastern Igbo springs, most of it was probably met from there until lately. The other dispersed Igbo whose land still supported agriculture had the need for the tools, (hoes and machetes), cooking utensils etc. that were produced by the smiths and potters of the Northern Igbo plateau. The movement of these minerals must have helped to stimulate the further development of exchange economy among the Igbo. Thus the development of an exchange economy among the Igbo did not have to wait for the contact with Europe in the sixteenth century, nor did the rise of specialist businessmen who lived in part from promoting such exchange.

In fact, a study of the Igbo-Ukwu finds made by Professor Thurstan Shaw *(1970)* would seem to reveal that by the ninth century A.D., Igbo land was already engaged in long and short-range exchange business. Long-range exchange brought in such items as the horseman hilt, carnelian beads from markets in Sudan and beyond. The short-range or regional exchange helped to assemble the slaves and ivory which paid for these luxury goods, as well as in collecting the worked bronze. According to Shaw, it was unlikely that all the bronzes were cast in Igbo-Ukwu, though surely from its distinctive style, it was cast east of the Niger and south of the Benue. The assembling of all these masterpieces from the master-craftsmen of the period would suggest a well-developed network of regional trade. *(In Afigbo 1975)*

During the 'Oil Rivers' normal trade, people of Igbo-Ukwu travelled as far south as Opobo, Calabar, and brought home flint guns, gun powder, textiles, spirits etc. The famous stop-over markets of *Eke Obinikpa* of Arondizuogu and *Oye* Okigwe were very well known to our people. *(Ike C. O. 2009 pg. 39)*

The middle men specialization followed with the contact with Europe and during the slave trade era. These trade specializations have been sustained in Igbo culture till date. I was opportune when I was younger to witness my grand-mother in the late 70s and early 80s as she prepares for an *Nkwo* market day business. She usually left for the market very early, before day break, with many empty baskets, loaded one in the other according to their different sizes. On rare occasions did she left the house with money or food crops such as bunch of plantain or fresh palm nuts taken from the farm for sales in the market. But each time she returned from the market, she came back with the baskets fully loaded with market gifts and food items she bought from the market together with ingredients for making soup that will last till the next *Nkwo* market day. It baffled me as a child what this woman went to do in the market each market day that brought her so much money. Not until I learnt that my grand-mother was a specialist middleman in palm products business *(Iwu-akwu),* that I came to understand why she left the house so early on a market day. She specialized in intercepting small products of palm, buying them off the producers and putting them together to make large collectives and then selling them off at a much higher profit to dealers, usually coming to *Nkwo* from far distant places, that process the palm products in different forms for consumption or for industrial usage. This is a typical of the business acumen that was developed by Igbo people and had sediment in them over the centuries. This well-developed ancient practice is what the Igbo people have carried on the modern days.

3
APPRENTICESHIP AND COMMUNITY CONSCIOUSNESS

The Igbo man like many other African nations is community conscious. Wherever an Igbo man may be, he keeps an eye at home and will always want to associate with his people that are around him. The Igbo cardinal belief that *"Aku lue uno, o lue ikwu na ibe"* meaning that the wealth that reached home is the only wealth that is valued by your relatives, makes it an imperative to an Igbo man that no matter the amount of wealth he has acquired, it made no sense if he has not invested any good chunk of it in his community.

Ottenberg's statement is a strong indicator of the Igbo man's attachment to his community. This attachment is based very strongly on kinship and family. The African brotherhood, *Ujamaa* in the word of Julius Nyerere or *Harambee* in popular Kenyan parlance is deep seated in Igbo culture. In 1939 Leith-Ross doubted whether the Igbo could visualize a world unrelated to the idea of a family. The highest level of this attachment is the clan *(Umunna)*, village group, or what Leith-Ross would call the *'Igbo state'*. Above the African brotherhood that is deep-seated among the Igbo, there is yet another elaborate form of kinsman ship; *nwadiana,*. *Nwadiana* is the mother's family link that automatically grants the children of a woman certain rights and protection amongst her brothers and in her father's family. In some dialects or cultural areas it is called *'nnaochie'*, *'ikwunne'* or *'umunenne'*, but they generally stand for the same tradition and practice.

The Igbo man views his family in relation to other families, and his person in relation to other individuals in the community. A successful man does not inspire respect if he fails to help the members of his family, especially the young, to make their own success. In this vein, the wealth of a man is not just valued on the volume of money or property that he has acquired, but also by the number of people he was able to train or raise in his business. The wealthy people have the mandate to take young people from the family or the community, train them over a given period of time and settle them in the terms of setting them up with capital and conducive environment that will help them to grow in the business. It is therefore understood that an Igbo man does not give his brother fish; he rather teaches him how to fish. The young man on the other hand has to undertake that period of training as a period of servitude and loyalty to his master. The understanding that *"Onye fechaa eze, eze eluo ya"*, meaning that he who serves a king loyally, deserves a kingship reward at the end.

In a similar manner, a community that is evidently lagging behind in comparison with others soon becomes an object of derision to its members, even if as individuals they are very successful. It is however not a mere flight from shame that makes the Igbo attached to his community. There are both social and religious reasons for this attachment. On the social level, the individual is indebted in many ways to the different levels of his community for his success. Again his community remains his last refuge. It is therefore almost natural that he should be concerned with the well-being of his group and its members. *(Oguejiofor J.1996)*

On the religious aspect, based on the eschatological worldview, when an Igbo man dies, he cannot be committed to any other mother earth except the home town or the home community where his ancestors were committed. No matter what the odds might be, like in the case of an air crash or distant death like in abroad for which the corpse cannot be returned home. The funeral of such a person cannot go on unless the ritual of cleansing, picking the soil from the place of the death and performing the rightful ceremony of burial rites before the funeral can go on; the absence of any of which the soul may not rest in peace. This very belief and practice killed the idea of cemeteries that were introduced in Igbo land by the missionaries in spite of the Igbo people embrace on Christianity.

To further buttress this fact, G.T. Basden observed that, "The desire of every Ibo man and woman is to die in their own town or at least, to be buried within its precincts. For a long period it is very difficult to persuade a man to travel any distance from his native place and if he were in need of medical assistance an Ibo would seldom agree to go from home in spite of assurances that he would be able to have better treatment elsewhere. In the case of death occurring at a distance, if it can be done at all, the brethren will bring the body home for burial." *(Basden, T. K. 1966 pg. 116)* In this regard, many Igbo immigrants choose to retire to their home village when they can no longer continue to work.

The Igbo people seek every opportunity to link with his clan and community. This is the very reason why many Igbo people would not miss to travel home during important celebrations, like Christmas and new yam festivals that attract very great mass returns in every Igbo community, also is the 'August Meeting' for their women. To this effect, therefore, the Igbo man seeks the development of his community and sees to it that his community is placed on the map of the State, Country or the World depending on the outreach or connections within the person's disposal. One negative impact that the exodus of Igbo people leave on their host community in Nigeria when they travel for such festivals is a kind of temporal devastation by desertification especially on cities where they dwell in numbers. Such exodus has often exposed the weaknesses of the hosts and the strangle hold on the city's economy by the Igbo people.

Due to distorted perceptions of this practice, the Igbo has been charged for clannishness, he is accused of unduly favouring his kindred and running to their defense at all times. He is supposed to have a tribal caucus where decisions are made and conspiracies hatched to advance Igbo interests. Such pan-Igbo solidarity is a figment of the Nigerian imagination. *(Achebe C, Op. cit.)*

The Igbo link to his community must however not be misconstrued as tribalism – if for nothing else, for the mere fact that the traditional Igbo ethos of hard work and competitiveness has almost necessarily given him a deep sense of fairness. *(Oguejiofor J. 1996 pg. 21)*

"The Igbo towns compete among themselves for certain kinds of social achievement, like building of schools, churches, markets, post offices, pipe-borne water projects, roads etc. They did not concern themselves with pan-Igbo unity nor were they geared towards securing an advantage over non-Igbo Nigerians. Beyond town or village, the Igbo have no compelling traditional loyalty." *(Achebe 1983 pg. 47)* The kind of loyalty the Igbo command is the kind that compels an Igbo man to ask at the first instance at meeting with another Igbo he is meeting for the first time; what part of Igbo are you from? If the answer coincides with the questioner's part of Igbo origin, he is more excited and may question further to the extent of asking; who is your father if the coincidence continues, but dies abruptly if there is a remarkable distance. Such a question might not even come up at all if there are marked distinctions in the dialects.

Analysis and current perceptions have shown that compared with their major competitors in the

Nigerian context (the Yoruba and Hausa-Fulani), the Igbo are the least equipped traditionally for tribalism or ethnicity – the undue preference for a person from one's ethnic group over another person in the conferment of something viewed as advantageous to the receiver. *(Oguejiofor J loc. cit.)* It is in accordance with this fact that Horton wrote of the Igbo in 1886, 'There is not that unity among them that is to be found among other tribes; in fact everyone likes to be his own master.' *(Horton 1975 pg. 352)*

4
IGBO SOCIETY AGE GRADING SYSTEM AND TITLE SOCIETY

The Igbo societies are arranged in such a way that there is an age grading system that works alongside other social structures. The age grading system sees children born within a range of three to five years lumped up into an age group that is usually identified with a name which may be coined from the extraordinary event of that period of their birth. These age grades are expected to do certain things together as a group when they are growing; such activities as learning a group dance or performing in wrestling match during events.

The age groups are also supposed to be the torch bearers of the community against other communities at certain stages. For instance in times of wars, the particular age grades that were ripe enough for war were expected to defend the community.

Elizabeth Isichei described the age grade in the following words 'This organization is in different grades, each being made up of young men of the same age. Each group took a name and appointed the eldest of them as their head. These age grades perform both civic and military duties in the town. They acted as the night watchmen of the town, when threatened by rogues. They also did public works, like clearing the forests and making local paths and roads. These age grades also were charged with guarding public morality through censorship of their members' behaviour. In most cases, they were the people who enforced the decisions of any judicial council.' *(Isichei, E. 1978, pg. 73)*

The age grading system had other effects that it imposes on the members which are positive attributes for growth. The members of a certain age grade are expected to do certain things at certain stages of their lives; the age of independence from their parents, the age of marriage, the age of building and owning a house etc. The member is supposed to move along with his or her age mates without which he or she is being looked upon as a failure. In the Igbo popular parlance it is said that, *"Ogbo onye wua ngige, anya ato ya n'ngige",* meaning that if someone's mate jumps a wall; he focuses on that wall until he is able to jump it.

This system has the effect of keeping the members continually competing and striving to achieve whatever a member is able to achieve regardless if the person has some distinctive talents. The society on its own part reminds and encourages the age group on when the group is ripe for certain activities such as joining the masquerade cult, owning personal farms, marriage etc. The competitions also cuts across communities, for instance, an age grade would seek to replicate a beautiful dance that was performed by a fellow age grade in another community or even aspire to do more than that. They wrestle against each other in gatherings and social events and compete healthily in virtually everything good.

The age grading system also has the effect of drawing a line for the community who are the spectators and the judges for passing judgment. A parent whose child is lazy or slow will always find a worthy example from among the child's age grade while trying to work the child up. The child by mere seeing his or her mates getting involved in marriages or in modern society, passing through schools or buying cars and owning businesses, knows automatically that he or she is being left behind.

Iwa-akwa or *Iwa-ogodo* (meaning covering with cloths) is a significant stage in the life of any age grade. It is the stage when an age grade is officially permitted to cover-up the body because they are judged to be transmitted into adults. It is usually marked with elaborate ceremonies and is the rite of passage of an age group into man-hood. Each person is shown his own plot of land that he is meant to cultivate and later build a house for the sake of raising his own family. The responsibilities are kept alive before him by the system.

"During the Igbo-Ukwu ceremony of '*Iwa-Ogodo*', all the pubescent males assembled naked at '*ikilikili*' to receive their first loin cloths from their parents. These were tied round their waists and crossed between their legs, leaving the ends to dangle like John Ploughman's cloak. The initiated young males, who by this rite of passage were regarded as taxable adults capable of taking part in compulsory and communal *'Olu Ugwu Okpu'* at Agulu, danced round the market and jubilated. They were given presents of scimitars *(obejili)*, swords and cutlasses. Children of the rich and influential people also got presents of guns." *(Ike C. O. 2009 pg. 174)* Girls receive their presents from their families at marriage. They receive symbolic gifts like the mortar *(ikwe),* kitchen knife *(mma-oge),* stool *(okpoga),* vegetable seeds etc.

The age grade system may not be very much in vogue in the various Igbo communities as it was in the past but the sediment effect of this view of the society is very much alive in the Igbo man and in every Igbo community. This is what has partly inculcated in an Igbo man the desire for achievement and also to keep an eye on a timeline on every achievement that he must make.

The title society is a social class in the Igbo communities that signifies honour and prestige for achievement. The title society is open to any person who can pay the price, with only the exception of the *osu*. They usually assumed the position of clan heads. The clan heads are essentially important personages in the political structure of the Igbo. Prestige could be achieved by wealth and good service like when we look at the prestige and honour acquired by Okonkwo in *"Things Fall Apart"*, at a youthful age. The highest qualification for a political post however, particularly for the council of the elders is age.

"When Unoka died he had taken no title at all and he was heavily in debt. Any wonder then his son Okonkwo was ashamed of him? Fortunately, among these people a man was judged according to his worth and not according to the worth of his father. Okonkwo was clearly cut out for great things. He was still young but he had won fame as the greatest wrestler in the nine villages. He was a wealthy farmer and had two barns full of yams, and had just married his third wife. To crown it all he had taken two titles and had shown incredible prowess in two inter-tribal wars. And so although Okonkwo was still young, he was already one of the greatest men of his time. Age was respected among his people, but achievement was revered, as the elders said, if a child washed his hands he could eat with kings. Okonkwo had clearly washed his hands and so he ate with kings and elders." *(Achebe C. 1965)*

The title group also provides bond, which bound different clans together. The *'Ozo'* title distinguishes the noble from the commoners and is a qualification for political appointment in a town. The title groups bear different names in different localities such as *'Ozo'* for Awka area, *'Ama'* for Nsukka area, *'Okpala' 'Eze', 'Nze', 'Ume', 'Obi', 'Dim', 'Ichie'* etc. but they bear the same structure. All titled men are therefore politicians and may be popular or unpopular in the council of elders. They could be used politically to test the popularity of the council.

The title group is generally distinguished in a gathering by the distinctive attire that is exclusively embellished with a red cap. A non-title man cannot put on a red cap in the public in his community. A non-title man cannot dance to the *uffieh* drums. The titled group also enjoys certain accord of respect in other communities especially when they visit other communities as a representative or just to participate in an occasion like marriage ceremony.

"Among the Igbo, the social title system is the one potent means by which a man's wealth could be translated into social and political statuses." *(LeVine)*.

To belong to the title group and to merit the prestige is the aspiration of every young Igbo man. This ordinarily builds the drive for achievement in him.

5
AMBITIOUS, HARDY AND HEADSTRONG

This is one of the distinguishing attributes of the Igbo people that have made them successful in all the things they get involved. The Igbo people have developed this attitude probably because of the population pressure that was intense with this people right from time which had forced competitiveness on the people. Professor M. Echeruo described this Igbo character in the following terms: "'Headstrong' and 'ambitious'. No two words can better define that quality in Igbo character which has been its primary source of strength and disaster. We are a headstrong people- sensible but headstrong." *(Echerue, M. 1979 pg. 23)*

When Ezeulu in Arrow of God, sent a message to the white man "You must first return, however, and tell your white man that Ezeulu does not leave his hut. If he wants to see me he must come here. Nwodika's son who showed you the way can also show him" he meant every detail of it until he was taken captive.

Even in captivity he remained proud and defiant. When he was tossed with the offer of being elevated to the position of chief of his clan, he replied, "Tell the white man that Ezeulu will not be anybody's chief, except Ulu." *(Achebe C. Arrow of God 1971)*

The Igbo man is rarely driven to an act. Most often, it is the headstrongness that manifests itself more clearly to an outside observer of the Igbo people. Clarke, the white man that was delegated to approach Ezeulu, "confronted with the proud inattention of this fetish priest whom they were about to do a great favour by elevating him above his fellows and who, instead of gratitude, returned scorn, Clarke did not know what to say. The more he spoke the more he became angry." *(Loc. cit.)*

Starting with earlier confrontations with the European slave traders, the slave traders never had it easy with the Igbo slaves. The *Olauda Equiano's* case is a classic example. The strength and quality of the Igbo slaves still made them preferable and priced higher in the market than other slaves especially compared with those of the West Indies. A 17th century French slave dealer made the following statement about the Igbo slaves which illustrates the number of Igbo people that were sold to Europe and North America; "This place (Bonny) is the wholesale market for slaves, as not fewer than 20,000 are annually sold here; 16,000 of whom are natives of one nation, called Heebo, so that this single nation has not exported a less number of its people, during the last twenty years than 320,000 and those of the same nation sold at New and Old Calabar, probably amounted in the same period of time to 50,000 more, making an aggregate amount of 370,000 Heebos." *(Isichei 1977 pg. 11)*

Onyekwere Dimkpa, writing about the Igbo slaves of Virginia Maryland who were recently honoured by the State for their contributions in the growth of the farm wrote; "Indeed, this honour is very fitting, as Virginia was dominated by Igbo slaves taken there during the trans-Atlantic slave trade. Indeed, a cursory look at the history of the trans-Atlantic slave trade shows that though they were considered rebellious and 'suicidal' by plantation owners, preferring to die rather than be enslaved wherever they found themselves during the slavery period, the Igbo quickly bonded and usually attempted to free themselves from the slavers' shackles. It is a fact of history that the slaves who fought off the Spanish and French slavers to found present-day Haiti had been mostly Igbo slaves who hijacked the vessels trans-shipping them from America to Latin America and headed for Barbados."

"The ex-slave writer Olaudah Equiano was among the slaves that were later trans-shipped to Virginia from Barbados. About 44 per cent of the 90,000 Africans in Barbados were from the Bight of Biafra from where the Igbo were shipped. There is even a story that could be apocryphal about the mass-suicide of a shipload of Igbo slaves on landing at an American jetty in November 28, 1858. Rather than disembark in their chains, the slaves were said to have jumped into the ocean instead. This event led to this particular jetty being referred to as the 'Ebolanding'." *(Onyekwere 2010)*

Oguejiofor wrote on the stubbornness of the Igbo, 'The manifestation of the Igbo stubbornness assumes more acuity to the person who is not accustomed to the Igbo character, and comes from a background which helps little to improve his adaptation or comprehension. It is therefore not surprising that a good number of colonialists saw little more than the stubbornness of the Igbo.' On the one hand, the fact that the Fulani had already established an Islamic hegemony over the north of Nigeria, and the Yoruba and the Bini had established feudalism in the west, made these parts of Nigeria better equipped to absorb the impart of the white man's colonialism. The Igbo people on the other hand, had a different and more painful experience. Ojukwu writes: "From the first impart of the white man's arrival, because of the misconstrued perception that the Igbo were product of lower, not just different civilization, all contact between the people – whites and the Igbos – took on an aspect of confrontation." *(Odumegwu Ojukwu 1989 pg. 130)*

For instance, the prelude to suppressing any community's uprising was to disarm its citizens. In Igbo-Ukwu in 1902, the chief announced that everybody would surrender his gun at Nkwo the following day. The announcement ended with the threat that those who failed to handover their guns would be handed over to W.A.F.F. On the fateful day, a mountain of old guns was built on the very spot where we have *'Ogbo-Ogili'* now. With everybody looking with consternation and dismay, fire was set to the guns. The white man stayed to supervise/watch them burn to ashes. The fear of arm uprising was thus removed. *(Ike C. O. 2009 pg. 75)* This episode is popularly known as *'Ntiji-Egbe'* and was experienced by virtually every community in Igbo land around this time.

Perhaps because of this confrontational approach, it was very difficult for the colonialists to establish effective control of the Igbo interior. Where it was possible to colonize a wide area of an Islamic state by simply signing a treaty with the emir or defeating his army in a single war, the British in Igbo land had to engage town after town and village after village for the simple reason that each of these constituted a city state, with an independent government which recognized no exterior masters. "As late as 1906, there were part of Igbo land which no white man has seen, and British control over the subdue areas was anything but secure and complete. *(Isichei E. p.136)*

It is no wonder that Igbo land was special problem for the white man. In 1909, Col Kemal wrote that Igbo land is really a small portion of Nigeria… But it has been the most troublesome section of any and the richest. As late as 1937, the British anthropologist, C. K. Meek, was congratulating the colonial administration on its progress in Igbo land which for him constituted the most lawless part of Nigeria.

From the benefit of hindsight, there is doubt that the description of Igbo land as lawless by some colonial official originated from their lack of goodwill or even perspicacity to study the people they were colonializing. This lack led them to many grievous errors, including the imposition of chiefs on a people who generally did not recognize chiefs in their traditional political organization. *(Oguejiofor J 1996)*

It took the excessive goodwill and good work of the missionaries and the conviction of the Igbo to turn things around. Nevertheless, there remains a strain of stubbornness that has been observed in the Igbo character by many other people including the missionaries themselves. The missionary J. Dennis was perhaps expecting a cringing attitude of the Igbo of Awka when she visited the town in 1899. She was disappointed and noted that all carried themselves with a dignified air, or perhaps more correctly sort of swagger, as though the entire world belonged to them. *(Isichei E. 1977 pg. 205)*

Before her, the pioneer missionary, Archbishop Crowther, had been disturbed by the attitude of the Igbo people, which he considered a 'great drawback', describing as 'something approaching lawlessness' their moral conduct. Here one sees again a disappointed expectation. Crowther certainly preferred a more docile and more controllable flock, but found the Igbo very independent. His view is corroborated by Basden (another missionary) who described the Awkuzu people of Anambra as 'a truculent crowd'. Among the non-missionaries, there is the example of the agent of the Royal Niger Company in 1890 characterizing the Obosi people as 'a wild and savage race of cannibals and apt to be troublesome.' *(Echerue 1979 pg. 13)*

It would be recalled historically that Obosi community, as recorded by Achebe, was the community that arrested the first white man that ventured into their community. For his colour and the shoes the man was putting on they assumed that he had no toes and as such was not human. They assumed 'it' to be and called 'it' a 'white pig', 'killed it and skinned it'. Assuming its bicycle to be an 'iron horse' took it and tied it to an iroko tree in case it returns to tell the stories and invite their members. In retaliation, the Royal Niger Company where the white man came from, surrounded the Obosi people on a market day and almost wiped out the whole community with rain of bullets.

This perception of the Royal Niger Company agent marked the relationship of the company with Igbo communities. The company official did not show themselves to be less troublesome, and their destruction of whole communities on flimsy reasons hardly showed them less wild or savage than the Obosi people. *(Oguejiofor J. 1996)* This was perhaps what informed the *'Ntiji-Egbe'* (disarmament) strategy which the white man used to subdued other Igbo communities.

Apart from the *'Ntiji-Egbe'* episode, there was also the phenomenon popularly known as *'Oso-Oyibo'*, (the white man's race). *'Oso-Oyibo'* in Igbo-Ukwu refers to the period around 1920 when the people almost took the laws into their hands because they were indirectly protesting against the warrant chiefs that were molesting them especially in the recruitment of labour. Igbo-Ukwu had been fined two hundred pounds under the collective punishment ordinance of 1915 for her citizens taking the laws into their hands.

Igbo-Ukwu ignored it and refused to pay the fine. The confrontation developed until on February 3, 1920, when a detachment of only sixty soldiers from W.A.F.F. under the command of Captain H. Jones arrived at Igbo-Ukwu and camped at *'Azudo'*. Meanwhile Igbo-Ukwu was holding an emergency meeting in the town hall at *Amaehulu* from where they rose to meet the soldiers at *'Azudo'*, not so much to fight them as letting them know their grievances, why the soldiers were sent and who sent them.

The soldiers at Azudo having been wrongfully informed by the chiefs' spies that the people of Igbo-Ukwu were assembling at *Amaehulu* preparing to fight decided to meet the people there at *Amaehulu*. The two groups met. Captain Jones gave a brisk command. A volley of shot was fired into the crowd. One Mr. Anaenyeonwu dropped motionless; a number of people were wounded. And others fled. *Oso-Oyibo* has started. *(Ike C. O. 2009)*

Some Igbo writers in diaspora have also observed the headstrongness of the Igbo people. James Africanus Horton, a Sierra Leonean born of Igbo recaptive parents, wrote in 1868 that "the Egboes cannot be driven to an act, they are most stubborn and bullheaded, but with kindness they could be made to do anything, even to deny themselves of their comforts." *(Horton J. 1975 pg. 352)*

It is interesting to observe how the Igbo character survived in many Igbo ex-slaves, even after the passage of time and a good measure of acculturation. Thus another Sierra Leonean medical doctor commenting on an Igbo grandmother wrote: 'she brought into our family the sturdy nonchalance of the Ibos.' *(Cole 1960, pg. 14)*

Sturdy nonchalance, stubbornness, in conjunction with other characteristics, has made the Igbo people very often feared and sometimes hated by other Nigerians. *(Oguejiofor J. 1996) 'Ibo Granmoun'* of Haiti Igbo has survived up to date and means that 'Ibo know no authority'. But on the other hand, this quality has made the Igbo very successful and able to subdue every predicament.

Their headstrong or stubbornness informs their attitude of never giving up. Even those of them who fail in business would never quit. Without capital they engage in what they call *oso-ahia* and can survive on it until another opportunity for a settled business present itself. This is one of their strong impetuses for success.

6
CLANNISHNESS, AGGRESSIVENESS FEAR AND INDUSTRY OF THE IGBO WOMEN

The famous African writer and Igbo novelist, Chinua Achebe, in his booklet, The Trouble with Nigeria, devoted a chapter to the Igbo people: The Igbo Problem. The Igbo are a problem, real or imagined, to the rest of Nigeria. "Nigerians of all ethnic groups will probably achieve consensus on no other matter than their common resentment of the Igbo. They would all describe them as aggressive, arrogant and clannish. Most would add grasping and greedy (although the performance of the Yoruba since the end of Civil War has tended to put the prize for greed in some doubt.)" *(Achebe C. 1983 pg. 45)*

It may be an over-statement to speak about the Igbo generally as clannish but it is undisputable that the Igbo people are clannish in business. Being clannish in this sense has helped them create miniature empires and controlled some or all the aspects in any trading or market they venture into. An Igbo man does not give his brother fish; he teaches him how to fish. They bring their relatives and young ones into their business as apprentices and set them up in the business after some years of education. The apprenticeships they build through the years help them to control markets effectively as a group. A particular city in Nigeria for instance may be dominated by traders or business men from one particular part or village in Igbo land. Likewise is every trade line in every city, like motor parts, textile, electronics etc. dominated by particular clans or towns in different cities in Nigeria and beyond. This is because; Igbo people in their clannishness continually bring in people from their homes and introduce them into this clan. They quickly fit into the clan and before you know it, they have a success history. In their noisy and arrogant behavior; they begin to exude their arrogance, by lavishly spending and living ostensible and boisterous lives. They also quickly incur the hatred and resentment of their host.

Besides bringing people from their home community and introducing them into the clan, the Igbo people also clan with the existing Igbo people in the place where they live, regardless of what home community they come from. The basis of the clan depends on the number of the Igbo people there and sometimes on the distance from home. They may just clan as one Igbo community if they are not so many, or they clan on the basics of State of origin, Local Government of origin, town or village meetings depending on the size of the population in that locality. The Igbo people go as far as establishing kings or leaders of their clan in every big city of the world that they dwell in great number. They create such title positions like of *Eze-Igbo* n' Abuja, *Eze-Igbo* n' Lagos, *Eze-Igbo* n' South-Africa, *Eze-Igbo* n' London etc.

There are other activities that were perceived as forms of clans among the Igbo people. The 1930s saw the rise of Igbo unions in the cities of Lagos and Port Harcourt. Later, the Ibo Federal Union (renamed the Ibo State Union in 1948) emerged as an umbrella pan-ethnic organization. Headed by Nnamdi Azikiwe, it was closely associated with the National Council of Nigeria and the Cameroons (NCNC), which he co-founded with Herbert Macaulay. The aim of the organization was the improvement and advancement (such as in education) of the Igbo and their indigenous land and included an Igbo "national anthem" with a plan for an Igbo bank. *(Uwazie, E. E. 1999, pg. 11)*

The subsequent ban on independent political activities after the civil war meant that Igbo people adopted other modes of clans in the form of clubs like the popularly known *"People's Club of Nigeria"* expressing the fact that this natural propensity cannot be taken away from the Igbo. The ban on political interest groups was only lifted in 1978 by O. Obasanjo's Military Government and we saw the formation of *Ohaneze Ndi Igbo* organization, an elite umbrella organization which speaks on behalf of the Igbo people.

However, "The rise of the Igbo in Nigerian affairs was due to the self-confidence engendered by their open society and their belief that one man is as good as another, that no condition is permanent. It was not due as non-Igbo observers have imagined, to tribal mutual aid societies. The 'Town Union' phenomenon which has often been written about was in reality an extension of the Igbo individualistic ethic." *(Achebe, C. loc. cit.)* Besides, being *Eze-Igbo* in Abuja or Lagos does not vest on the title holder any recognition in his home community. He may not put on the red cap within his home land until he has taken the official traditional title of his home.

Achebe adds that the origins of the resentment are, among others, "the danger of hubris, 'overweening pride' and thoughtlessness which invites envy and hatred' or even worse, which can obsess the mind with material success and dispose it to all kinds of crude showiness." Furthermore, he contends that there is in them "noisy exhibitionism and disregard for humility and quietness." *(Achebe C. loc. cit.)*

Taking these attitudes in the Igbo person in isolation is partly the reason Igbo man has been grossly misunderstood even by himself. In fairness, some Igbo intellectuals would choose to add that these negative traits may be like giving a dog bad name in order to hang him. Practices and ethos in Igbo society like Igbo worldview, age grading system, title society etc. which have engineered the Igbo progress and successes also naturally spawn some attitude in the Igbo person. Since the Igbo society despised failure and sometimes over-praised success, it is quite natural that every member of this society who is successful, will seek the least opportunity to announce to his people and to the world, in the words of Achebe, that "'he has made it' and is desperate to be noticed and admired." This is what has made the quiddity of an Igbo.

It should seriously be noted that no Igbo man makes merriment when he has a project in his hands. When he has a project like expanding his business capital, building a house, saving to buy a car or to marry a wife etc. he does not make merriment in the *'Owambe'* party style of western Nigerians nor does he portend the *'Ba Kwomi'* lifestyle of the northerners. He does merriment at the end of an achievement to show his people that he has arrived. We must therefore eschew sentiments that those attitudes arouse while attempting to understand the Igbo person. The background from where these people are coming from should be put fore-most into consideration. There are therefore other Igbo intellectuals that are of the view that envy and jealousy explain why the Igbo people are so perceived by other Nigerians. *(Nwabueze 1985 pg. 8)*

No people in the world possessing something close to the dynamism of the Igbo have received good credentials from their neighbours, especially when these neighbours find themselves dwarfed by the toughness of their competitors. Much can be said here on the experience of the Jews in Nazi Germany, and in Europe in general throughout history and presently against the Arab world. The same applies to the Berbers of Morocco who are viewed much like the Igbo by a good number of their Arab compatriots. *(Oguejiofor J. 1996 pg. 17)* The Germans are the other case in Europe.

One may begin to wonder at this point what role fear has played in the success of the Igbo man. Fear here is not the fear of death or the other but the fear of failure. The fear of failure is intrinsically present in the life of an Igbo. The society builds this into him.

Aigboje wrote in his commentary on Things Fall Apart that, "Okonkwo's prosperity was visible in his household and beyond it. What nobody knew was that this famous man was leading a life dominated and motivated by fear of failure and weakness like his father, and fear that the reputation and wealth he had built up would pass on to a worthless son, Nwoye." *(Achebe C. 1965)*

Okonkwo ruled his household with heavy hand that is inspired by fear. Most times the Igbo demonstration of wealth and success comes from that urge to demonstrate and prove to his people that he is successful. This is a propensity that is derived from his background, just as Okonkwo's demonstration of strength is an outcome of fear which lies deep within him for the fate of his father. Unfortunately when this wealth exhibition is done in foreign lands, their hosts see nothing but arrogance and boisterousness.

The Igbo people are also parochial with regard to marriage, more or less like the Jews. The other Nigerian women get into relationship with some Igbo men with utmost suspicion and would mostly do that within a temporal perspective just for fun or the purpose of getting some chunk of his wealth. This is simply because she is convinced that the man would dump her and rather marry an Igbo woman in the end. And this is often the case. The Igbo man's parochial in marriage should rather be seen as a boost to his success in business, for an Igbo woman will always bring to the family that attitude of hard work, sturdy nonchalance, stubbornness, in conjunction with other characteristics of the Igbo people.

An Igbo woman would always hold her ground. It is the culture that men own farms which they cultivate and weed with their wives and family, but the woman own the cultivation of certain crops in the farm, cassava, coco-yam and other vegetable crops to be precise. This traditional practice gives the woman certain level of economic independence and control. The woman used the proceeds from these crops to support her husband and family substantially. The practice had created in the Igbo woman the habit of industry. The social and economic independence it gave to the woman made it a desirable opportunity for the woman.

In modern Igbo societies where agriculture has ceased to be the means of subsistence but rather businesses, the Igbo woman would seek the same opportunity for economic independence and self-determination through the establishment of her own business. In most cases they demand for it and the husband may not have peace, directly or indirectly until he has done well enough to get the woman established. Other Nigerians and people who may not understand the basis for this attitude of the Igbo woman and whose culture do not encourage such freedom rather fear to marry an Igbo woman.

Captain Hugh Crow made great remarks about the Igbo women and their industry which made them preferred by the plantation owners in America during the era of slave trade. Thus, "the Eboes tho' not generally robust types are a well formed people of the middle stature: many of their women are of remarkably symmetrical shape, and if white, would in Europe be deemed beautiful. This race is, as has been already remarked, of a more mild and engaging disposition than the other tribes, particularly the Quaws and though less suited for the severe manual labour of the field, they are preferred in the West Indian colonies for their fidelity and utility, as domestic servants, particularly if taken there when young, as they then become the most industrious of any of the tribes taken to the colonies." *(Crow H. 1970 pg. 198)*

Such remark by Captain Hugh Crow does not only make allusion to the industry of the Igbo women but also buttresses her beauty and some element of lust by the white people for Igbo and African women. Many stories of the European colonial masters taking Igbo women to bed during the colonial era amidst holding strong racial discrimination abound.

Apart from their industry, Igbo women usually grouped into *umuada* and *inye-ma-ona* are a powerful group. The attempts to set up warrant chiefs in the predominantly republican Igbo land came to grief in the late 1920's and led to the wide spread turmoil and rioting by women, known as the Aba Women Riot (1929). This failure showed the nature of the Igbo government and the freedom and power that their women enjoyed. The people did not look upon the warrant chiefs appointed to represent these areas as their representatives since the idea was alien to them.

These warrant chiefs exploited the powers vested upon them by the British and acted rather as despots and tyrants. The people on their own part were not accustomed to such leadership that they could not control. The Igbo usually appoint their own representative who must speak for them or be boycotted. They resented taxation because it would be used to provide salaries for the despotic Chiefs.

The idea of taxation was also unfamiliar to them, fines from defaulters and occasional for a purpose being the only traditional method of raising communal funds known to them. It was ridiculous that innocent citizens should also be levied, worst still when the colonial government extended taxation to women. It was never heard of and the women instantly did not tolerate that.

Igbo people have produced some of the strongest women leaders in Nigeria with the likes of Prof. Dorathy Akunyili, Dr. Ngozi Okonjo-Iwuala, Ndi Okereke Onyiuke and a host of others

7
HARD WORK, FAITHFULNESS AND DESIRE FOR ACHIEVEMENT

One of the important attributes of an Igbo man that has engineered his success is his attitude to work. The Igbo man believes in success through hard work and to that effect, he is aggressive at work. One of the earliest of such observations must be that of Olaudah Equiano, who published in 1789 a book entitled *The Interesting Narrative of the Life of Olaudah Equiano or Gustavaus Vasa the African.* On his people's attitude to work, Equiano wrote: "We are all habituated to labour from our earliest years. Everyone contributed something to the common stock, and as we are unacquainted with idleness we have no beggars. The benefits of such a mode of living are obvious. The West Indian planter prefers the slaves of Benin or Eboe to those of any other part of Guinea for their hardness, intelligence, integrity and zeal." *(Equiano O. 1967 pg. 7)*

It is absolutely correct that in the traditional Igbo society, there were no beggars. It was intrinsically considered as evil for someone to be a beggar and they were detested in the community. Everybody work to avoid this evil. The common thing was that the relative bankroll an unfortunate or backward person in the family as often as they can and as long as the person did not continue to misbehave or indulge in laziness. It is a common believe that *"Nwanne onye ara ka ifele na eme"* it is the relatives of a madman that gets ashamed and not the madman. This inspires the move to get the madman off the street. You may not be considered a rich man when your brothers or relatives around you are poor.

However, it should not be understood that Igbo would not ask for help or support from someone who could render such when they need it. An Igbo for instance may not feel any remorse or humiliation to ask someone for water. Water in Igbo is one of the commonest materials and no matter how the scarcity might be; he would never refuse a visitor water at least to drink. In the same vein he believe that while in a strange land, he may not ask for anything but water; part of the reason why Igbo people in the Nigeria context were some time in the past called *'inyamili'* by the northerners. The origin of this terminology being that most Igbo people that came to Northern part of Nigeria after the amalgamation could not speak the language but would always confidently walk up to their host and say *'nye m mmili'* meaning 'give me water.'

An expatriate Irishman Robert Collis wrote about the Igbo; "Many expatriates have found the Ibos easier to work with than the men of other tribes in Nigeria. I, myself, found them very pleasant work companions. They had a greater capacity for hard work than most and could grasp the significance of what they were doing very quickly." *(Collis, R. 1970 pg. 46)*

Oguejiofor observed that there is, of course hardly any culture that does not in certain ways encourage hard work as a human weapon for the domination of nature. The case of the Igbo people is extraordinary. The testimony of many writers has confirmed a somewhat extraordinary concern of the Igbo people for hard work. In 1881, the British Vice-Consul on the then Oil River Protectorate described them as 'exceedingly industrious.' *(Isichei 1977 pg. 200)*

Writing further, he observed that it is possible that Isichei was right in noting that the adulatory description of the Igbo by the Consul (Johnson) was a sort of stick to beat the Niger Delta middleman, coming as it did at the time the British wanted to side track them in order to have direct trading relations with the Igbo interior. However an indication of Igbo concern for hard work is that in some Igbo communities, one of the powers of the *Okpala* (the eldest man of the kindred) is to drive a noted lazy young man out of their kindred. *(Meek C. 1937 pg. 121)*

Commenting on this trait, Nwoga writes of the Igbo that 'no work is too hard to be attempted; no job is menial to be used in the struggle with the world for achievement. *(Nwoga D. 1984 pg. 66)*

Indeed the impetus towards hard work is the desires for individual achievement. There are titles and various statutory positions in the community, but the criteria for ascendancy into such hierarchy are basically personal achievements and achievements for the good of the community. Apart from the *okpala*, age does not determine any position. Anybody can be admitted into the council of elders or *ozo* society depending on your achievement. Okonkwo in *Things Fall Apart* is a classic example. "He was still young but he had won fame as the greatest wrestler in the nine villages. He was a wealthy farmer and had two barns full of yams, and had just married his third wife. To crown it all he had taken two titles and had shown incredible prowess in two inter-tribal wars. And so although Okonkwo was still young, he was already one of the greatest men of his time. Age was respected among his people, but achievement was revered, as the elders said, if a child washed his hands he could eat with kings. Okonkwo had clearly washed his hands and so he ate with kings and elders." *(Achebe C. 1965)*

The Igbo desire for achievement is somehow singular, given that the Igbo people give deference to achievement not linked to inherited position. *(Ojukwu 1989 pg. 95)* This may be a side effect of the fact that in Igbo land there are really a few such positions, securely reserved for individuals or families by the mere accession to which they gain automatic status, "*Nwa nwa tote otokwulu*". It is of course, good to have some inheritance, material or otherwise, from one's forebears. But among the Igbo, such inheritance must be backed up by personal achievement if it is not to slide into disrepute. A son of an *ozo* title holder cannot dance the *uffieh* music because his father is an *ozo* title holder unless he too is elevate into the *ozo* society. He cannot inherit his father's *ozo* title-ship even when his father is late.

It is not a credit to anybody to have your wife's dowries paid for by your father or brother. You must work to earn the power and right to marry a wife and pay the bride price along with any other responsibilities that are involved. In the circumstance where your father or relatives had to do that or render some helping hands, you must have the absolute responsibility of raising and fending for your family. It is said that: '*anaghi a lutara mmadu nwanyi, bunyekwa ya ute*' you do not marry a wife for someone and also provide the mat or the bedding for them to make love.

The Igbo desire for achievement is one of the major reasons why they are resented by other Nigerians. And perhaps this quality is what must have been misinterpreted as 'grasping' and 'greedy' as recorded by Achebe. Ottenberg wrote that the Igbo people are described by non-Igbo Nigerians as pushing or aggressive and that this is a result of their concern for strength and achievement. *(Ottenberg P. 1965)* These are quite hasty conclusions on the Igbo people that were generally reached commonly by other Nigerians and the colonialists.

There are legends of men who have started from extremely humble beginnings and made it to the top without losing touch with humanity and charity. One person worthy of mention here is Olaudah Equiano. Equiano is probably the first Igbo writer, and wrote his autobiography about 1789. The book was written in French and later translated into English as "The interesting Narrative of the life of Olaudah Equiano or Gustavus Vassa the African" or simply called "Equiano's Travel".

As indicated in the narrative, Olaudah was born about 1745 to an Igbo clan. He narrated the beautiful life in Igboland before he was kidnapped together with his sister and sold into slavery. Passing from one hand to the other, he finally came to the hands of his eventual master, a Frenchman who was a sea captain, he re-baptized him Gustavus Vassa and he remained in his hands until he was able to buy his freedom through hard work. He was quite intelligent, energetic, hardy etc. just like a typical Igbo man. His exposition as a ship captain's slave benefited him so much. He gave himself reasonable education and proceeded to write his book in which he attempted to give the world the true image of Africa and the ugly face of slavery.

Another person is the story of the Igbo genius slave, born Jugbo. Jugboha from Amaigbo, Nkwerre Imo State, later known as King Jaja, began life as a slave in Bonny, graduated to a canoe paddler, successful trader, and, ultimately, head of the House of Pepple and finally became King of Opobo; a king not to be surpassed. The Saga of Jaja so charmingly written up by de Cardi (1899); Dike (1956); Jones (1961) etc., illustrates the Igbo at his best: courageous, adventurous, hardworking, charitable, obstinate, proud and faithful to his friends and benefactors.

Other notable examples of Igbo people who achieved great wealth and greatness through hard work in the 50s are the late Sir Odumegwu Ojukwu and the late middleweight champion of the world Dick Tiger. Sir Odumegwu Ojukwu from Nnewi, Anambra State, started life as a petty trader, rose to an ex-produce inspector, a multinational businessman, a transport magnate, a banker, a financier, and, finally, a Knight of the British Empire. The late Mr. Dick Tiger Ihetu from Nkwerre-Orlu, Imo State, started as a bottle picker and retailer at Eke Oha, in Aba Township in 1951-1952. Within this time he entered boxing and rose to become world middleweight champion before 1960. Tiger was also a businessman, a school proprietor and a Member of the British Empire (M.B.E.).

Many Igbo elites of the past and present have similar stories of coming from being nobody to where they are today. And this is because of the Igbo society that encouraged such developments. The sky is no limit to any Igbo child today that is dreaming of getting to any level, provided he is ready to work it out through the genuine means. He will have the support and prayers of his fathers.

Sometimes also the Igbo man may just work for the sake of getting busy. "From the age 9, while still in primary school, Chukwuemeka engaged in petty trading; selling matches and soap bought for him by the mother. He pushed truck and did other menial jobs not out of necessity. Mr. Chukwuemeka Ezeife was a Pupil Teacher, The Salvation Army Primary School Igbo-Ukwu 1954-1960." *(Dr. Chukwuemeka Ezeife on his autobiography, 2012)*

An average Igbo-Ukwu man and generally all the people of the Northern Igbo Plateau where the lands no longer support agriculture would go to farm not necessarily for the purpose of making profit nor for the fun of it but because he would not want to be viewed as a lazy man. Sir S. B. Obikwelu would lament bitterly how futile it was cultivating the little pieces of land behind his home. Yet he could not stop this process in spite of his being a well-paid Civil Servant. Annually, he would go to the *Nkwo* market to buy some yam tubers for cultivation, stressfully work on the farm throughout the year, harvest the yams successfully and tie all the harvest in the barn. Barely eating any tuber from them, he preserves them for cultivation the next season; yet he would still have to go back to *Nkwo* to buy more tubers to supplement at the next planting season.

It should be emphasized however that the traditional Igbo man was not simply concern with achievement and pursuit of wealth. These pursuits must also have some moral basis. Traditional Igbo society had severe penalties for dishonesty, an almost logical follow-up to their dedication to hard work. Wealth acquired under dubious circumstances does not earn respect; it has to be earned through hard work, under conditions of integrity and without deceit. *(Okigbo 1986 pg. 19)*

What applies to wealth extends to other modes of achievement. *(Oguejiofor J. 1996)*

Oguejiofor wrote that the Igbo concern for hard work and achievement tends to leave them with little patience for the lazy and for failure. Sylvia Leith-ross, an English anthropologist, whose work reveals a remarkable incomprehension of the Igbo, was at least correct in saying that the Igbo reserved the purest scorn for the lazy and the incompetent. *(Leith-Ross S. 1939 pg. 49)* Laziness and untimely failure invite public contempt, being counterforces to the quest for achievement.

But failure that comes after gallant hard work is rather viewed with sympathy, *"O mebelu ma chi ekweghi, onye uta agaghi ata ya"* meaning he that set forth to achieve, but destiny or the gods says otherwise, should not be blamed. What is derided is failure due to indolence and laziness. Even your own children may deride you. Okonkwo in *Things Fall Apart* derided his own father and hated poverty with aggression because of his father. An event he would never want to remember was that his lazy father, Unoka, was thrown into the evil forest at death because he died of a swollen stomach; a disease considered to be evil in the community and to have come to him because of his poverty.

One Igbo man was said to have been inquired from by his children, where he was when all the rich men around him were making all the money. So poverty is not a thing any Igbo man would want for any reason to be associated with. It is evil for a man to die *"enwe nta enwe imo"* leaving behind neither property nor wealth. Because at death, the level of ancestor-ship that one joins depends on the position one occupies and the level of wealth that he leaves behind. The level of ancestor-ship that deserved sacrifice on regular basis is the most desired; the sacrifice of cow, goat, fowl, yam etc. depends on the individual's wealth capacity. The case of Obiakor the strange one in Achebe's *Things Fall Apart*, who consulted an oracle and got the reply that his dead father wanted a goat as sacrifice. The young man defied the oracular message of his father by retorting, "Ask my father if he had a fowl when he was alive?" *(Achebe C. 1967 pg. 30)*

It is important to dilate here on the eschatological worldview of the Igbo. The Igbo believe that after death, one joins the ancestors but not before a befitting burial right and funeral have been conducted. The kind of ancestral spirit one becomes depends largely on the person's personality during his life time. It is believed that '*Onye ka mmadu n'ndu, ka ya n'mmuo'* He who is greater than one in life is equally greater than and ahead of him in the spirit world. Therefore the hierarchy one attains in life is maintained at death which ultimately keeps the destiny of an Igbo man in his own hand and for while he is alive.

He struggles to earn a good life so as to guarantee a happy death. He also struggles to beget children, especially male children because of his believe in re-incarnation, *ino-uwa*. If one did not beget a male child, it is not possible for him to be re-incarnated into his family which is the most desired. Possibly he would be re-incarnated into a daughter's family or a strange family in the case of no issue at all. This situation is what the Igbo would not want to find himself and hence struggles on and even go as far as marrying more wives to beget a male child. In spite of the fact that Christianity has thrown a different light on eschatology, many Igbo people still stick to this practice and in most cases, ignorantly.

The Igbo belief in re-incarnation somehow presents an antinomy which many Igbo do not realize. How was it possible that the Igbo continue to consult and pour libations on the spirits of their ancestors that they already believed to be re-incarnated and is living there with them? The Igbo haven been Christianized may not be bordered again by these traditional beliefs but the impacts of these traditions are very much still around him propelling him like a force, making him seeking to achieve.

The modern Igbo trader would never rest from Monday to Saturday. He only closes his stall or business in the night because there are no more customers coming in and on Sundays, for some religious obligations that has been imposed on him by his acceptance of the Christian Religion. This is understandable because there is nothing like holidays or break hours in the traditional Igbo work period. This is due to an age long culture of working in and out of season. The Igbo behave the same way in the employed labour sector. It is not an over-statement to say that most of the private enterprise owners in Nigeria would prefer to employ an Igbo in that area where a lot of industry is required.

The quality of industry is gleaned from being traditionally habituated to labour. The Igbo man agriculturist would leave his home with his family before cockcrow in the morning and without breakfast headed to his farm. The man with his family would work in the farm throughout the day only to return at sunset and taking their breakfast sometimes as brunch within the work. In some cases, the families migrate and settle temporarily in the farm site through the farming season. Sometimes they rotate between farms. Some of these farm settlements eventually turned into permanent homes to the migrants and accounted for many of the migrations in Igbo history. This habit is what the Igbo have carried along with him even as he embraced European culture.

The white-collar job in one sense has not served as a substitute to the Igbo industry. The Igbo work to reap the benefits of the white-collar job even as he is not ready to leave his farm work or business. In most cases, you find many Igbo people who double as a Government worker as well as an after-work or weekend businessman. Most Igbo people that travel abroad also exude this habit of taking to more than one job, one for the morning, one for the after-noon and sometimes another for the night-shift; to the amazement of their hosts, usually the western world and to the embarrassment of other Africans. He works with the focus on acquiring enough wealth to free him one day but in his very nature would not stop working after freeing himself.

In 1789, Olauda Equiano, an Igbo ex-slave who, with the inherent traditional Igbo spirit of enterprise, worked in the day and studied in the night to free him from both physical and mental slavery. The Igbo students in Europe or America or anywhere in the world in the modern day feel the urge to double as workers even when they do not need it because they are from very wealthy families and have enough support from home.

The other important thing about the Igbo man in business is that he is faithful to his friends and benefactors; he is also faithful to his clan's business ethos. The Igbo man with his forward looking perspectives would never want to severe a relationship with any customer or even just a potential customer. In most cases, people would prefer to do business with them because they remain faithful to the terms of the contract and would keep the business secret to the later. They build very good and open customers relationship.

The clan's business ethos would make them behave in certain ways that eschews interference in other peoples businesses. In some of the business clans, there are strong disciplinary measures that deter people from intruding or interfering with other people's affairs or business. No matter how greedy one may be, Igbo people are mostly faithful and loyal to the laid down rules and principles in their business clan. They may cluster in one business and in very small portion of a market and compete among themselves, but they respect their rules especially when dealing with the customers. They bond easily to get the best of a customer.

8
COMPETITIVENESS, CONFIDENCE AND ABILITY TO TAKE RISKS.

"The rise of the Igbo in Nigeria affairs was due to the self-confidence engendered by their open society." *(Achebe C. op. cit.)* One of the societal endowments for hard work among the Igbo is their competitiveness. It is an attitude that shows itself primarily in the social structures like the age grading system and in the inter-communal relationship. The Igbo child or man is continually conscious of his position and achievements in relation to the members of his age grade. He is propelled by this system that creates a healthy rivalry and forcing each child to carry along and not to be left behind. The parents and relatives also help to ginger and inspire courage and confidence into a child that seemed to be lagging behind.

On the other hand also, every Igbo community has a deep consciousness of its position in relation to the neighbouring communities. The independence of these communities is taken for granted, but there is always a strong rivalry between neighbouring communities. *(Green M. 1964)* Sometimes the rivalry is between related communities. In the past this often led to inter-community violence or war. The spirit of competition was also found within single Igbo communities in which sections were often at loggerheads with one another in the process of balancing out the use of power and the administration of justice. In the Igbo individual, therefore, there is also an ingrained sense of competition. This attitude has been nurtured in many ways by such structures as age grade and title societies. There are certain basic things which a capable person is expected to do at the appropriate period with the members of his age grade. Title societies are open to whoever, except the *Osu*, can pay the price.

Even those that are assumed icons in distinctive positions are not safe from challenges. There is no timidity or reluctance of younger people to challenge positions staked by older people assumed to be icons of the community in Igbo culture. A person for instance may be of world highest reputation but he may have to face very stiff opposition in his home community in Igbo land. *E si be ya eje be onye?* Everyman is held in equality. There is no man who does not see the moon from his own compound, but this does not mean that he is denied of any due respect.

In recent time this attitude has been developed enormously and has helped immensely in the development of Igbo land. The primordial consciousness of the image of the group, which crystallized into similar attitudes in the psyche of the individual, has received a great booster from contact with European culture, which is 'essentially competitive.' The new outlook it assumed is aptly described by S. Ottenberg as follows: "Villages compete to build the first or the best school, village groups to improve their markets. Many social groups strives to push some of their sons; ahead in schooling and to obtain scholarships in competition with other groups. Individuals who acquire schooling, wealth, or political influence are expected to use their new social standing to benefit the groups with which they are associated." *(Ottenberg S. 1959 pg. 138)*

It is necessary at this point to modify the impression that this account of Igbo inter-communal competitions might have so far given that the different clans are always in loggerhead with one another. They are not really always at rivalry. Many clans are exogamous, which means that men must marry from outside the clan. Thus, one clan was bound to all the surrounding clans by inter marriage. Age grades tend to undermine the independence of a clan because people of the same age over a number of clans may hold more loyalty to their age groups than to their clans. A good masquerade or dance is repeated in different clans as a mark of respect or a goodwill visit to the clan's heads. Other clans may deliberately invite the group during festivals or to teach them the dance. The practice tends to unite the clans. Again, wrestling contest, hiring of good drummers, flutters and trumpeters has strong binding effect on the clans, so do secret societies.

The other product of the competitive spirit is an inherent ability of an Igbo man or an Igbo child to undertake risks. The society encourages the child to do what other children in his or her age grade had done or is able to do even though they may be of disparate talents. The desire for achievement and determination to succeed creates in the Igbo man that urges to take unimaginable risks to the amazement of other Nigerian nationalities.

Okeke writes in his autobiography, "He encouraged all his children to work hard and gave us opportunities to engage ourselves in money-yielding ventures. I still remember that at about the age of eight, I followed my older brother, Emma and his mates, Micah Emenike and Godfrey Ihebe to trek twenty miles to Onitsha to sell bundles of broom, spices (uda), coconut and a few other items...my parents refused because of my tender age. I pestered my father to let me go and when he noticed my dogged determination to join them, he gave in. He personally helped me to package my brooms and I got a sizable quantity of "uda" (local spice) to make up my ware...the long trek first took us to the boundary of Oba and Obosi and we passed the night by the road side. Thereafter we set out early in the morning to enter Onitsha around 7.00am.... after selling our wares, we entered one restaurant and ate to our hearts' fill and drank coca-cola, a rare drink for us in those days. We then took stock of our incomes and were set to return home. It was then that it was dawned on everybody that I could not make the long trek back because my feet blistered and ached terribly. One Mathias Odiefe, a worker in a nearby mechanic workshop came to our rescue. He put me in a lorry which took me home to Amichi the same day while others continued their long trek back." *(Okeke S. N. 2006, pg. 31-32)*

To the Igbo man, no job is too menial and no profit is too little. He can work the length and breadth of his life for just a little profit and sometimes just for the purpose of getting busy. The migration of the people also offers them the opportunity always to start a new life and to work up the ladder in a new profession when he has being considered a failure in another. The streaming host of Igbo people looming all the cities of the world may not have that ease of comfort but they stay on with the determination and that positive perspective that they will someday make it. The Igbo also believe that the more wealth one has, the more the one is able to undertake even higher risks. *"Aku na esi obi ike"* that wealth is a source of courage and confidence.

Sir Rex Niven wrote; "the Ibo have the same courage and intelligence as the Irish and they had not come under any greater authority than the village nor had they encountered an outsider in the war-path. Every man has always been for himself and has usually done well himself. Under the new administration they now had to look over their shoulder; they were no longer alone. They lapped up education when it came their way; they took up the learned professions and did very well in them. They filled important professional and technical posts all over the north. They traded and worked with commercial firms with success." *(Niven, R. 1970 pg. 18)*

9

EGALITARIAN INDIVIDUALISM MANAGERIAL QUALITIES AND ASTUTENESS

"The Igbo derive their spirit of individualism from the structure and organization of the simple family or compound family units. The units encourage individual achievement within the communal context of the *Umunna* units. In other words, Igbo individualism is based on the structure of the *Umunna*." *(Ogbalu F. C. and Emenanjo E. N. 1975 pg. 89)* Individualism is a state where a person tends to assume independence from other people in his actions. The Igbo are comparatively very individualistic, and this observation leads face to face to what has been rightly termed an *antinomy* in the Igbo character: 'balancing the strong individualism of the Igbo and his fierce loyalty to the village and community.' *(Okigbo op. cit. pg. 14)*

Many observers have marveled at the range of Igbo communalism and individualism and how they could co-exist. On the personal level, they are noted for their self-confidence and for the strong conviction that one person is as good as another, *"isi ka isi bu n'onu"* that one head is greater than the other is a matter of speech. Ethical principles are very strong. One short but meaningful Igbo proverb says: *Egbe belu ugo belu, nke sili ibe ya ebena, nku kwaa ya.* Live and let live. A warning that good has to be done otherwise something tragic would happen. *(Ifesieh E. 1989 pg. 196)*

In their interpersonal relationships, the Igbo people are not noted for cringing servility or sycophancy. This is greatly in contrast to the other nationalities in Nigeria like the Yoruba that go as far as prostrating in front of an elder when greeting and the women to the men. Very often this trait in the Igbo man has been misconstrued as lack of respect, a blatant misconception, given the fact that the Igbo are taught from their earliest childhood to respect all who are older than themselves, and to have deep respect for the elderly. *(Okigbo op. cit. pg. 15)*

The ethos of individualism greatly coloured Igbo economic organization. It is described as economic individualism. Yet mutual help is not lacking among the traditional Igbo, both in the tillage and weeding of their farms, in erecting living houses and in repairing them; in directing or instructing an inexperienced person how to get about in the pursuance of his business and in the training and apprenticeship of specialists like diviners and smiths. However, over and above the assistance accorded to the individual, he is expected to be able to fend for himself, especially if he is blessed with good health. A mature and married adult is expected to fend for his family, and it is a source of confidence for him that he is able to do so. Economic individualism and independence is thus another impetus to hard work. *(Oguejiofor J. 1996 pg. 22)*

Children were trained in working with their parents in their farms, business or craft. They continued to do so until the approach of adulthood. They were then given their own portions of land and yam seedlings, and were expected to develop them through their efforts. The same procedure largely applied to those sections of Igbo land which specialized in occupations other than farming. Most times in specialized crafts like smiting, herbal medicine, oracle running, *ichi* carving, etc. the child takes after his father. This is what the Igbo has incorporated into the modern day apprenticeship whereby the master at the end of the apprenticeship or service, sets off his pupil with some capital and other necessary environment that will enable him to succeed as an entrepreneur. Somehow, this attitude is lacking in the Igbo behavior in the Government circle or the Civil Service, and presents a real situation where the antinomies in Igbo individualism and communalism co-exist. The Igbo would help to train a relative in school and even finding a job in public service, but the tasks of growing and sustaining in this job is left almost absolutely to the person.

The Igbo found the incorporation into the wider context of Nigeria as an opportunity for their economic individualism, aided by a spirit of hard work, to blossom and this was considerably achieved.

It is not often surprising the quickness with which the Igbo, who were traditionally assumed by early European Anthropologists to be agriculturists, and therefore sedentary, have also become notable for their business acumen. Davidson remarks that 'these people have always enjoyed a reputation for restless enterprise in trade.' *(Davidson B. 1969 pg. 92)*

T. K. Basden observes that the Igbo are 'astute in trade' *(Basden 1966 pg. xi)*. But it was Okigbo that seems to be more perspicacious in writing that the rise of the Onitsha market as the largest market in West Africa 'reflects the prime activity of a people restless and active, dedicated to improve their lot by self-effort rather than by charity.' *(Okigbo op cit. pg. 17)* It is the force towards self-improvement that has pushed the Igbo to make some breakthroughs in some otherwise almost impossible condition. They do not in any case wait for the Government to provide amenities or to maintain and advance on the one they were privileged to have.

Economic individualism which gives rise to segmental and atomistic organization has not been all too advantageous in the modern situation where unity promises far more than atomistic organization. In fact, it is a major disadvantage in the Nigerian context. Still the Igbo have largely stuck to their traditional system in spite of changing and harsh Nigerian circumstances. Disadvantageous as this may be, it seems to be confirmation of deep-seated Igbo individualism. Each person wants to convince himself and others of his personal capacity. He wants to see his success as a result of his labour, not that of some gigantic impersonal conglomerate or of the contribution of friends and relatives. This attitude on the other hand has made the Igbo completely progressive.

It can thus be seen that Igbo economic individualism underlines the Igbo concern for personal worth. We have noted earlier that inheritance is considered a fortune, but that, in any case, the inheritor has to show himself to be a capable person. In Achebe's *Things Fall Apart*, Unoka, Okonkwo's father's lack of success did not stand in the way of Okonkwo to pre-eminence. Achebe rightly pointed out that he owed such a phenomenal rise both to his hard work and perseverance and to the ethos of his clan. *"Nwata mara kwocha aka ya, o solu ikele rie nri.* When a child is able to wash his hand clean, he is admitted to dine with the elders. In many places, Okonkwo's historical background would have constituted an albatross to his admittance to the hall of fame. But this is not so among the Igbo: "Fortunately among these people a man was judged according to his worth and not according to the worth of his father." *(Achebe C. 1988 pg. 20)*

Igbo individualism should not be misconstrued as opposed to the practice of banking in Igbo economics. Igbo banking was more in the nature of savings and loans. The Igbo savings and loans invention is popularly known as *'Isusu'* in which contributions are pooled weekly or monthly and one person, who has the need, or whose turn it is in a rotational balance collects the fund. This is still very much in practice in Igbo land today and in many colonies where Igbo people clan in numbers. Igbo slaves took this invention to the Caribbean Islands where they still practice it and call it "*Sue Sue.*" They also put the use of such fund to their advantage.

With this sort of banking system already in existence among the Igbo, the Igbo are not afraid to borrow. It is not surprising how the Igbo understand very well the modern banking system of borrowing, making some business venture with it and repaying as quickly as possible. Most often than not, they are able to repay within the stated period, because they understand how crucial it is to the future of the business and their ability to borrow in the future. Installment repayment is best in their favour since this is exactly the same modus operandi of *isusu.* The banks are the ones in trouble to ensure that the repayment of their money is guaranteed.

On another hand, an average rich Igbo businessman is intelligent and a good manager. He may not have gone to any school but the skill in keeping records of accounts and goods in an omnibus store is not easy to come by. In most cases, the Igbo traders make use of the crudest methods of keeping track records of goods and their values and in linking with other markets to correspond with ever changing market values. Sometimes what other people think to be useless, they placed values on them and someday, those values become meaningful. We see a lot of this with those of them who deal on used motor spare parts and other second-hand items.

Igbo people had a way of keeping record of debts and debtors. Unoka in *Things Fall Apart*, had a way of keeping record of his creditors, though he made ridicule of the whole system by applying it in a negative sense. "Look at that wall', he said, pointing at the far wall of his hut, which was rubbed with red earth so that it shone. 'Look at those lines of chalk;' and Okoye saw groups of short perpendicular lines drawn in chalk. There were five groups, and the smallest group had ten lines... 'Each group represents a debt to someone, and each stroke is one hundred cowries. You see, I owe this man a thousand cowries. But he has not come to wake me up in the morning for it. I shall pay you but not today. Our elders say that the sun will shine on those who stand before it shines on those who kneel under them. I shall pay the big debts first.'..." Okoye who had come to collect the two hundred cowries Unoka owed him rolled his goatskin and departed. *(Achebe C.1965 pg. 6)*

A mathematical calculation among the Igbo is not a difficulty. This is due to an age long tradition of mathematical calculations of monetary values. The Igbo mathematics that is usually used in calculating money is similar to the Roman numerals which makes it a little bit very complex and difficult. In the Roman numerical system, there are symbols like I=1, V=5, X=10, L=50, C=100, D=500, M=1000 etc.

In the Roman counting, I stands for 1 and II which is I and I or 1+1 stands for 2, 3 is I and I and I or I+I+I= III. 4 is remarkably not written as IIII but IV where V stands for 5 and a V with an I before it means V-I or 5-1 which is equal to 4, 4 is therefore written in negation to 5. While 6 is written as VI with an I after V standing for 5+1=6. Similarly other numbers like 9 is written in negation as IX where X is 10 and the I coming before it represent 10-1=9, whereas 11 is XI which is 10+1=11. 20 is written as XX but 40 is not written as XXXX but rather as XL which means 50-10= 40. This is a more complex form of counting and calculation. The more reason the world was quick to adapt the much easier Arabic numerical system even at the face of Roman imperialism.

The Igbo counting system is akin to the Roman counting system. There are absolutes in Igbo traditional accounting numerals like *Ofu-ego* = 1kobo, *Ego-iri* = 1 Naira, *Ogu-ego* = 2 Naira, *Ohu-ego* = 20 Naira, *Nnu-ego* = 40 Naira, *Akpa-ego* = 200 Naira etc. *Ogu-ego nabo* simply means 2+2 = 4. *Ogu-ego ise* means 2+2+2+2+2 = 10. *Nnu-ego nabo* means 40+40 = 80. While *Akpa-ego nato* means 200+200+200 = 600. *Ogu-ego ito na ego-ise* means 2+2+2 =N6+50k =N 6.50k.

The negation aspect comes in like the Roman numerals when you count closer to these absolutes. 38 Naira for instance is counted as *Belu ogu-ego n'nnu-ego* that is 40–2 = 38. And 180 naira is counted as *Belu ohu-ego n'ofu akpa-ego*. That is 200–20 = 180. In addition to the negation, there are other formats that involved a position for instance; 205 naira could be posited as *Uma-ego ise n'ofu akpa-ego* that is remainder five on 200. It is equally saying the same thing as to say 200 + 5 = 205.

These few examples, if they have not made this system clear, must have at least exposed the complexity of the Igbo accounting system. These rigors the Igbo went through certainly had sediment in the Igbo people for centuries. It explains the ease with which Igbo people come to grasp with any monetary system even without having to go to any school for it. It does not baffle then why Igbo people has great mathematical instincts. They have produced great mathematicians of International repute like Professor Chike Obi, Philip Emeagwali and a host of others. There are also the best of Economists and Financial Managers in the like of Professor Charles Soludo, Ngozi Okonjo Iwuala, Ndi Okereke Onyiuke, etc.

One popular king in Igbo land was noted for his astuteness in business when he offered one community that was in land dispute with another and was in the verge of losing it to buy off the land and the case from them and take whatever comes out of it afterwards. He secretly and independently also made similar agreement with the other community that also felt that they may be losing the land in the end because it did not belong to them in the first place. Both communities waited in vain afterwards to see their mercenary go into war with their enemy but that was never to be. By the time they realized what happened, they had both signed documents that peacefully ceded the land to the king, who is neutral and a stranger to both communities.

Another story that buttresses Igbo astuteness and sometimes shrewdness in business is that portrayed by a popular story in Nigeria of one Minister in the 80s who called for tender for a certain job in the Federal Ministry of Works. The first person to tender for the work was from the Western part of the country and he successfully defended his bill of 30,000 Naira for the job. The second person was from the North, he had some difficulties defending his bill of 60,000 Naira, but he was confident in the end that he will get it because the Minister was from the North. The third bidder was from the East or precisely an Igbo man. He had an outrageous bill of 90,000 Naira; the Minister only invited him for a defense for the sake of equity and fairness. In his defense, he said that he had such an outrageous bill because he has a carefully worked calculation for it. That 30,000 Naira is meant for the Minister, 30,000 Naira for the Contractor and the remaining 30,000 he will pass on to the man from the West to deliver the job appropriately. The Minister quickly signed the contract in his favour.

It is important to mention here therefore that the Igbo man in business is not always the good. Sometimes some people had used their business acumen to despicable goals. The Aro warriors in the ancient Igbo land were known to have used the *Ibini Ukpabi* cult to defraud other communities and sustain what was then known as Aro hegemony around Igbo land.

Emmanuel Nwude, former single largest shareholder and Director of Union Bank of Nigeria, is a notable advanced-fee fraud artist. He is most famous for successfully defrauding a Brazilian man, Mr. Nelson

Sakaguchi, a Director in Banco Noroeste Brazil, of US$ 242 million between 1995 and 1998. He was arrested and convicted of the crime, courtesy of some Nigerian leaders who hate the Igbo with passion but would not mind looting Nigerian treasury to the dregs and defrauding Nigerians.

Nwude voluntarily surrendered a majority of his assets in the settlement of the case. He was sentenced to 25 years in prison and Mr. Sakaguchi was returned the majority of his lost assets. According to Wikipedia, the scam was the third biggest in banking history, after Nick Leeson's activities at Barings Bank, and the looting of the Iraqi Central Bank during the buildup to the U.S. led invasion of Iraq.

10
DEMOCRATIC INSTITUTIONS AND FREEDOM OF THE INDIVIDUAL
(Ultra-democracy and Absence of Kings)

The Igbo people evolved a political system that is segmentary and ultra-democratic. It is a system that succeeded in rejecting hegemony as worthy goals in politics, a system founded on the political philosophy that large is bad and small is good. *(Ojukwu op. cit. pg. 127)* Observers have never ceased to wonder at the level of democracy which the Igbo consistently maintained among themselves. "So natural did it seem to find autocracy in some form or other wherever one went in Africa that it was impossible even to imagine a democracy so absolute as that of the Igbo." *(Leith-Ross op. cit. pg. 67)*

Ejiofor defined democracy as a form of government in which every member of the community participates in decision-making as of right and can contest for any office in the state. When a member may participate through representatives, the system is designated representative or indirect democracy. *(Ejiofor L. 1982 pg. 23)*

The Igbo democracy has also been noted to be one of the highest development of this system of government practiced anywhere in the world. Compared with the Greek city-states, they are similar in many ways but it surpasses the Greek democracy in many ways. It gave a certain measure of government power to women, and rejecting hegemony, assured that each community or state had the right to self-government. Compared with the China city-states, it is almost superior in a sense in that amidst the inter community competitions and antagonism; it is still able to maintain the African spirit of brotherhood, both within the communities and among communities. There were, of course, inter-community conflicts and wars. But as Uchendu has said, 'an aggressive expansionist policy does not have much meaning for the Igbo. Their expansion has been small and predatory.' *(Uchendu V. 1965 pg.20)*

One reason for this is that among the Igbo, political office was non-remunerative. To this day, this attitude has survived in the numerous development committees that exist in Igbo communities. They have the task of collecting contributions and donations from the members of the community (and not without paying their own share of the contribution or dues). The money realized is usually channeled to development projects, like building schools, post offices, town halls, rural electrification, granting scholarships to the young, etc. it is remarkable that the officers of these committees do not usually receive any emolument for the sometimes very difficult work they do. *(Oguejiofor J. op. cit. pg. 24)* The king or the political office holder has to do other works to support himself and his family. In most cases, kings and officers are elected not without taking into consideration the person's integrity and responsible financial capability.

Each Igbo community jealously guarded its independence and was not lacking in derogatory remarks about all other neighbouring communities. In return, it received similar remarks from these other communities. Thus the dominant mood among the Igbos,' says Afigbo,' was that of robust parochialism.' *(Afigbo op. cit. pg. 16)*

On the other hand, kings were rare phenomena among the Igbo; giving weight to the saying *Igbo enwe eze* (the Igbo have no kings). Even in the exceptional instance where there were kings, their areas of jurisdiction were limited to single towns or communities, with such possible exceptions as the king of *Nri* who exercised some sort of cultic or religious influence over a small part of Igbo land.

The colonial administrators made fundamental errors in attempting to create warrant chief to rule the Igbo people through them. Achebe writes; "Once the white man had crushed Igbo resistance it was relatively easy for him to locate upstarts and ruffians in the community who would uphold his regime at the expense of their own people. From those days the average Igbo leader's mentality has not been entirely

free of collaborating Warrant Chief Syndrome."
(Achebe, C. op. cit.)

Writings on the root of Haitian democracy have greatly reflected the influence of Igbo. "Although the word democracy is from Greece, the concept of democracy arose independently in other societies. It arose among the Ibo people of today's Nigeria, where people's right to have a voice in how they are ruled was respected. The ancient Ibo people of Nigeria had a democratic state. Unlike their neighbors, (in Haiti) the Nago, the Guedevi, and the Mayi, who were ruled by a noble class, the Ibo people were not ruled by monarchs. They had no kings, nor queens. The Ibo people were their own authority. Here in the song, this concept is presented as *Ibo Granmoun*, meaning the Ibos take orders from no one.

The Ibo people were ruled by a parliament called *Igwe*. This body was comprised of elders nominated from each *lakou*, the Haitian term for an extended family compound. As a result of this ancient Ibo democratic government, today there is a popular expression among the Ibo people of modern day Nigeria: *Ibo ama eze*, which means the Ibos are their own authority. Across the Atlantic, *Ibo ama eze* has been translated into Creole as *Ibo granmoun*.

Among the many Ibo influences present in Haiti, perhaps the most enduring is the Ibo passion for self-determination. That passion helped to fuel our foreparents efforts to combat slavery. As their descendants, we continue to honor the Ibo and all the other nations who fought to create a more democratic

Haiti. No Africans in Haiti were willingly enslaved and people of all African nations rebelled against slavery. Nonetheless, because of the Ibo passion for democracy, they became the group most associated with rebellion against slavery. As such, in Haiti, when we honor the memory of Ibo Ancestors we commonly perform dance movements symbolic of their breaking the chains of enslavement. In Haiti, this rebellious way of dancing is called the *Ibo dance*."

The Igbo personality is a miniature of a typical Igbo state where there were usually no kings, where there was absolute democracy, and where each person was convinced of his personal worth and guarded his autonomy very jealously while giving to others an equal measure of autonomy. Personal and communal autonomy was an impetus to hard work and hard work helped much to encourage fair competition. *(Oguejiofor J. op. cit. pg. 25)*

On another hand, some people have argued on the existence of kingship culture among some Igbo communities especially the people of the riverine area before the coming of the Europeans. Professor Ejiofor, after his studies on the kingship culture in a western Igbo clan, Ezechima, wrote "thus in Umuezechima, the political power resides manifestly in hierarchical institutions, but the power base is firmly with the people. It is a curious arrangement, which makes for a harmony of democracy and monarchy; it is evidence of the influence of Benin Kingship co-existing with Igbo democratic culture." *(Ejiofor L 1982, p.336)*

Elizabeth Isichei who also did her work on the western riverine area recorded from the Ibusa community that "in early times, Ibusa had no *Eze* title. No one was an *Ezeman*. But as time went on, one Ezechi had himself crowned the *Eze ofu ani Ibusa*, that is, he became a single monarch like those of Ogwashi, Ubulu-Ukwu and Benin." *(Isichei E 1977, pg. 55)*" There is therefore little doubt that typical Igbo communities had no single ruler or king." *(Oguejiofor J.O 1996 P.31)* The idea of kingship is a later import. A study of the Nri theocracy may also lay proof to this fact but perhaps the Nri people may have made some ingenuous inputs that evolved the culture the way it looked, likewise was the evolution of the Aro aristocracy.

The other democratic institution that existed among the Igbo people is the concept of "*Ora nwe eze* - The king belongs to the people" and not the people to the king. In '*Arrow of God*', a novel by Chinua Achebe, we see this concept contained in Nwaka's demagogy. The Igbo people know no king, "*Igbo Ama Eze*". This is true in a sense though some Igbo communities do have kings and certainly they all recognize certain specific roles, which are defined in the social structure, and they also recognize personal achievement. The expressions used by Nwaka to disregard the role of Ezeulu implied the understanding that "*Ora Nwe Eze*". In spite of the various roles and positions recognized by the Igbo, they are worth nothing outside the support of the people. Decision and policy making is still left to the popular opinion and not to any fiat by any king. This is the traditional democracy in the strict sense. Even the powers and authority of Ezeulu could not have been without the people's support.

"Yes, it is right that the Chief Priest should go ahead and confront danger before it reached his people. That was the responsibility of the priesthood. It had been like that from the first day when the six harassed villages got together and said to Ezeulu's ancestor, you will carry this deity for us. At first, he was afraid. What power had he to carry such potent danger? But his people sang their support behind him and the flute man turned his head. So he went down on both knees and they put the deity on his head. He rose up and was transformed to a spirit. His people kept up their song behind him and he stepped forward on his first and decisive journey, compelling even the four days in the sky to give way to him." *(Achebe, C. Op. Cit.)*

The role of the people in the king installation is made clear here and the breakdown of such support means a breakdown of the kingship or priesthood. But Ezeulu, at this level of conflict, seems to be contemplating within himself the limits of his personal powers, the temptation to constitute himself into an arrow of God, which is in conflict with the exigencies of public responsibility. Ezeulu was not really a king in the real sense. He was a priest, some kind of a theocratic ruler.

"He was merely a watchman. His power was no more than the power of a child over a goat that was said to be his. As long as the goat was alive, it was his, he would find its food and take care of it but the day it was slaughtered, he would know who the real owner was. No! The Chief Priest of Ulu was more than that, must be more than that. If he should refuse to name the day there would be no festival – no planting and no reaping. But could he refuse? No Chief Priest had ever refused. So it could not be done. He would not dare." *(Achebe, C. Ibid.)*

The climax of the novel Arrow of God comes when 'Ezeulu finds his authority under threat. He has rivals in the tribe, in the white man's government, and even in his own family. Surrounded by trouble, he adopts an increasingly cosmic view of events: surely, in the battle of the deities, he is merely an arrow in the bow of his God? Armed with such ideas, Ezeulu is prepared to lead his people on, if necessary to destruction and annihilation. The power of the people, however reasserts itself.'

There is therefore no contention against the Igbo absolute democratic principles. This democratic spirit guaranteed the freedom of the individual that was held in esteem. The democratic and individual freedom put together is one of the key reasons for which Igbo people were progressive right from time immemorial.

Another attribute the democratic freedom and competitiveness had endowed on the Igbo is his push for versatility. In order to meet up with challenges and the stiff competition, the Igbo seek to become versatile, either by himself or by his family. The head of a family would not want the entire family to concentrate in one city or on one profession. And he wouldn't mind if some members venture into unknown areas. Ezeulu dealt with this propensity in him and the forces against it when he affirmed.

"How does it concern you what I do with my son? You say you do not want Oduche to follow strange ways. Do you not know that in a great man's household there must be people who follow all kinds of strange ways? There must be good people and bad people, honest workers and thieves, peace-makers and destroyers; that is the mark of a great *obi*. In such a place, whatever music you beat on your drum there is somebody who can dance to it". *Ogaranya muba nwa, ya munye agafu, o muba nwa ya munye mbuba, ka o ga abu okwu sie ike mbuba e buru ya n'isi, ugwo toba ike, agafu eje natakwa onye ji ya. (Achebe C. 1977 pg. 46)*

CONCLUSION

The Igbo has continually presented himself as a big enigma to the world and his fellow countrymen in Nigeria and sometimes even to himself. The enigma surrounding the Igbo including his origin, worldview, character, wealth, inclinations etc. had often led to general misunderstanding of this people. The studies of this people from different perspectives seem to hold the key to bringing this people to a better understanding to the world. The Igbo development of great and successful business enterprises is only one window to studying this people. This study is good for the Igbo man who may cherish the understanding of himself and see a reason to continue to cultivate and advance some of his social endowments consciously, and to others who may want to emulate or learn from the Igbo.

The exhibition of high business potentials and acumen in the Igbo person is as a result of combination of many factors; the environmental factors, the socio-political system, the social and cultural values, skills development and transfer, religious and general worldview. The immediate and remote predicament of the Igbo in the Nigerian context has also played a significant role. A combination of these factors contributed in giving the Igbo man a distinctive character. The Igbo character almost offhandedly defines the Igbo attitude in every other endeavour.

Coleman observed that "Ibo land is one of the most densely populated rural areas in the world. In some places the density is more than 1000 persons to the square mile. Moreover, the soil is comparatively poor. As a result, in the past the Ibo expanded territorially and exported to other areas large numbers of seasonal labourers and even semi-permanent residents. In fact, the Ibo were expanding territorially in many directions at the time of the British intrusion. Since then this outward thrust has continued and has been the source of anti-Igbo feeling among the tribes bordering Ibo land." *(Coleman, S. J. 1979 pg. 69)*

The Igbo man was forced by his predicament to begin quite early enough to develop the high business acumen that has sediment in him over the centuries. They have continually put into use these skills and seem to be continually forced by their worsening environment (both social and physical) and Nigerian economy to develop further on them. This art of the Igbo man has made him very rich, self-reliant and able to surmount every huddle presented to him especially within the Nigerian context much to the despair of his counterparts. It was not an over-statement when Achebe declared that "Nigeria without the inventiveness and the dynamism of the Igbo would be a less hopeful place than it is." *(Achebe, C. op. cit.)*

It is said that necessity is the mother of invention but the Igbo business prowess was not developed just by necessity, but a combination of this and many other social norms and culture. A deeper understanding of these motives that lie behind the Igbo attitudes and behaviour, I believe, would lead to a better harmony and peace with the other Nigerian tribes and the peoples of the place in the entire world where the Igbo people live today.

The Igbo behaviour in the modern political setting in Nigeria has been particularly enticing. Claude Levi-Strauss in his work on Race and History studied the natural behaviour of politicians. He observed that "The political opponents of political system are disinclined to admit that the system can evolve; they condemn it as a whole, and would excise it from history as a horrible interval when life is at a standstill only to begin again when the interval is over. The supporters of the regime hold quite a different view, especially, we may note, when they take an intimate part, in a high position, in the running of the machine". *(Levi-Strauss, C. 1956)*

One may note how differently the three major ethnic groups in Nigeria react in this regard in politics. When the Hausa-Fulani lose out in a political campaign, they accept defeat, go home and begin to re-strategize on how to regain power by the next dispensation. When the Yoruba lose out in a political campaign or tussle for position, they stay around and employ every means to oppose and distort the incumbent; a typical of the scenario that Levi-Strauss painted. They go beyond that to scheme against the incumbent and seek means of getting him removed and taking over the position.

The Igbo complete this tripartite relationship with a surprising behaviour. The Igbo, when he lose out in a political struggle, do not get home to re-strategize or fight the incumbent, rather he seeks a way around to get involved in the running of the machine. And most often he achieves that and plays a very strong role in supporting the regime with his will, intellectual and creative capabilities. No government in Nigeria has succeeded without having Igbo people on the background running the technical parts of its machine. In the Banking industry, Ministry of Finance, Power and Electricity, Health and Drug Law Enforcement or any other department where the Government sincerely wants to make a positive impact or change, an Igbo man or woman is called in to assist. This is an aspect of the Igbo attitude that has brought tranquility and progress in Nigeria but which Nigeria has denied them recognition of this important contribution. They would rather regard them as quislings, traitors and dangerous.

On another hand, it is also interesting to note how this tripartite wedlock behaves when they are in power. The Hausa-Fulani when they achieve power, they first and fore-most surround themselves with their fellow Hausa-Fulani, but then gradually turn around to locate those of other compatriots that may be vital to the success of the regime and gradually bring them in, in most cases as delegations.

The Yoruba on their own part does the same thing as the Hausa-Fulani by surrounding themselves with their fellows. Quite unfortunate the Yoruba do not see any other compatriot in Nigeria as good as themselves and so they shut them out in the running of the regime. This crude tribal inclination made

Achebe to spare nothing in launching his disgust for the Yoruba in his work, *The Trouble with Nigeria.* However, this inclination, according to some writers, is gleaned from an inherent fear of the other doing to him what he is inclined to doing to the other.

The Igbo in his belief that one man is as good as another has a totally different orientation and disposition when in power. He is confident and believes in himself. He is not afraid of working with or bringing in any person into his surrounding no matter who you are. His egalitarianism and individualistic tendency propels him to attempt to achieve, and in most cases, given the opportunity, he is able to succeed. Under the fairly impartial colonial umpire he was appreciated for his competency and hard work, but in the subsequent Nigeria syndrome, where tribalism over-took competency, he was relegated to the background. The Igbo in power on the reverse faces the stiffer opposition from his fellow Igbo who are wont to feeling that he fails them by exhibiting his natural egalitarian and individualistic tendencies in place of carrying them along in a tribal conspiracy as other ethnic groups do.

One living example of this attitude of the Igbo I will mention in this work is that portrayed by Mr. Stephen Okechukwu Keshi. Without hesitation one may say that Keshi started the revolution in Nigerian football that brought about the golden years of Nigerian football in the 90s. Having gotten the opportunity in late 80s to play in Europe, he was not selfish or afraid of taking on any challenges. He exuded the Igbo man's egalitarianism by opening the door for many of his colleagues that played with him then for New Nigerian Bank FC and others around Nigeria to play in the Belgian league and later France, Turkey, Holland and other parts of Europe. Those players formed the pivot on which the National team was later to flourish. In the Super Eagles they called him the 'gaffer' because of his influences on almost all the players and on the team in general. He captained Nigeria to victory in Tunisia 1994 and also to the pristine qualification of Nigeria for the World Cup finals in USA later that year in which Nigeria took the world by surprise. In USA, as the captain still, he played only one match and willingly sat on the bench for the rest, allowing the younger players to get the job done. He superannuated to a directive position.

He was successively criticized after the World-Cup exit, and designated as leading a 'mafia' group in the National team. How would he not command a great influence in the team if he had single-handedly made most of the players in the team and the team itself? The result of the subsequent antagonism and marginalization ensured that the team was almost entirely disbanded. It was replaced by a much younger team that was made up almost entirely by the under-23 team that was victorious in the Atlanta Olympic of 1996, much to the disgust of the older boys. The result was the gradual and protracted death of Nigerian football.

The decline continued while Nigeria was busy banking on 'expatriate' foreign coaches and on some incompetent locals and could not qualify for the World-Cup and the African Nations Cup in 2006.

While Keshi once again went on diaspora and was employed by Nigeria's neighbour Togo, a Country of less than 20 million people where he rallied and qualified their rag-tag team for the Nations Cup and World Cup the same year. He later moved to Mali where he replicated the same feat. What could have informed the Nigeria Football Federation to eschew sentiment and appoint Keshi as the National Coach in 2012 is what I can't figure out yet and if he will be allowed the opportunity to continue what he is already doing with the National team for long.

Speaking on the National television he exudes the kind of infectious confidence and authority that infects Nigerians with confidence. He has in a short time turned around the National team that could not qualify for The Nation Cup just a year before. He has taken on-board many former Nigeria footballers from all parts of the Country to help build the National team. He has moved the focus on foreign based player to include local talents and is open on performance and zeal or chauvinism to play for the Country as the fundamental qualification for players to dawn the National colours, and not the part of the Country you come from or 'who you know'.

Without mincing words, it may be said that Keshi, with regard to what he is doing at the helm of the National football team right now, is an epitome of an Igbo man and what the Igbo man is for Nigeria.

(Keshi won the third African Nations Cup for Nigeria in South Africa in February 2013 as a coach, three months after the first edition of this book was published.)

EPILOGUE

THE TRADITIONAL IGBO SOCIO-POLITICAL STRUCTURE

For a better understanding of the Igbo traditional Social life to non-Igbo people, I have added this appendix taken from my previous work "Igbo Race, Origin and Controversies."

The Igbo are not only a proud race but also are highly political. They possess an advanced political system when compared with other African ethnic groups. The political system is segmentary. The chief political units are the title group, the age group (elders) priests, and secret societies. Each of these has a part to play in the traditional government of the Igbo. The people are immensely democratic with the result that decisions tend to be slow. Administration is by council whose functions can be legislative, executive and judicial. This is to say that there is no central organization among the whole Igbo and this also accounts for the hegemony of the Aro and the conquest and penetration by the colonial masters.

The Igbo are so fragmented that just one or more lineages made a clan. The lineages made up of smaller socio-political units. The basic socio-political unit is the Umunna, which is patrilineal. The Umunna may be made up of a number of extended families of family groups. The large families are in turn made up of a large number of nuclear families. The Umunna is headed by the Okpala, but with limited political power. He exercises control with other elders of the Umunna as a kind of primus inter pares in matters relating to the Umunna. In general, clan meetings or affairs, he acts as a representative for his Umunna. Usually, he may not interfere with other activities involving the smaller units within the Umunna unless he is invited to use his influence.

Most of the Igbo clans are heterogeneous while a few clans dwelling along the Anambra River claim to be homogenous. In all, a group of Umunna forms a village section (*Ogbe*) or a village itself. An aggregate of villages in turn constitutes a town or what in time is called an autonomous community. There are many such clans in Igbo land and they are to a large extent independent of one another. A number of clans with the same dialect make up a cultural area. Some of such areas are Awka, Nsukka, Owerri, Onitsha and Abakaliki. The extent of deviation in dialect depends on the extent of external influence. The clan heads are essentially important personages in the political structure of the Igbo. Prestige could be achieved by wealth and good service like when we look at the prestige and honour acquired by Okonkwo in "Things Fall Apart", at a youthful age. The highest qualification for a political post however, particularly for the council of the elders is age.

Government administration proceeds through the council. There are two main councils, the council of elders and the general council of all the citizens called *'Ama-ala'* or *'oha-obodo'*. The council of elders is the highest authority in town. It is composed of the representatives of the major segment heads of the lineages. The elders are looked upon as the fathers of the clan and are expected to protect the interest of the town. A clan has pieces of lands in different locations and the elders have to protect the boundaries of the locations. However, it does not only take age to belong to the council of elders, it also requires some form of good reasoning and wisdom, strength in war and farm work.

The council of elders also legislates on matters of land ownership, cultivation of crops, animal rearing, initiation ceremonies, supply of labour for communal work and marriage customs. Legislation consists of rules to preserve the tradition, check offences and avoid offending the ancestors. No taxes are imposed and the only source of income remains the fines imposed in forms of kegs of palm wine, goats, fowls, sheep and confiscation of other properties. The masquerade group carries out the function of enforcing the law and maintaining peace and order. Among the executive members, we have the priest and the elders. The priests are highly respected and feared because they are believed to be chosen by the gods. Their functions are mainly religious and to some extent political. They offer sacrifice for the people at festivals and they also beat drums for political gatherings and they announce the day of general assembly. A spectacular example of such a priestly role is the function of Ezeulu, the chief priest of Ulu as recorded by Achebe in his work *"Arrow of God"*. The office is not hereditary in most cases and the custodian is believed to be inspired.

At the council, one of the elders may be regarded as the senior political officer or the chairman. Any one of them could be delegated to deal directly with the elders of another clan council. Any one of them could be authorized by the council to be the speaker on a specific issue or to deliver the verdict or the opinion of the council to the general assembly. Usually, other elders will stand behind the speaker to show support and sponsorship. Any member could as well be selected to function as emissary or to carry the council message to other councils in other clans. Just as the case in *"Arrow of God"*, where Akukalia was selected by the people of Umuaro as the emissary to carry their message to Okperi people which turned out to be the crisis among the leaders of Umuaro.

Although the council does not sit without the citizens, it generally sits in public and the people might have a voice. Any man however, could sit with the elders particularly in matters that affect him personally. This measure is a check on the elders. Apart from that, if an individual is dissatisfied with the decision of the council, he could summon the general assembly of the citizens to express his views. If an unpopular decision was taken or if the elders are despotic, the general assembly is called and the citizens could bring the whole business of the town to a standstill through boycott. In "Things Fall Apart", the *'Egwugwu'* is the highest and final court of appeal. In chapter 10, we see the dispensation of justice among traditional clans as in the case of Uzowulu versus his wife. There are no lawyers and there are no liars. Judgment is based on true evidence. There is no play with legal technicalities. The *Egwugwu* is nevertheless a council of the elders under the cover of the masquerade cult. Okonkwo, for instance, as an *Egwugwu*, became an ancestral spirit. Nevertheless, his transparent nature is against the spirit of the court since the mask is meant to conceal the judges. Such practice eliminates favoritism; bribery and corruption, hence preserve justice.

Women *(umuada)* are also a powerful group. They can call the general assembly when they feel that the council or the men are neglecting certain things, which they ought not to neglect. The general assembly is normally called for cerebrations, sacrifices, announcements, hearing individual or group complaints and for development programmes.

The elders of the extended families, minor segments or the full council settle disputes. The settlement by the head of the extended families can be regarded as settlement in low court. The case goes from the plaintiff to the headman. He contacts the defendant and both appear on the appointed day, usually in the evening. The case may end here with or without fines imposed on the guilty party. If either of the parties feels dissatisfied with the settlement, the case would proceed to the high court.

The council of elders is the highest court of appeal. Cases reach it through the heads of the families or from individuals or group of people involved. Here the plaintiff and the defendant must appear if necessary with their witnesses. The elders may use age groups as messengers who carry the summons to the defendant. The major offences comprise theft, rioting, land disputes, irregular land lease, and neglect of agreements, obligations and divorces. The people are called together by the aid of town criers.

Land disputes dominate the list of cases. Agreements are not written and sealed as they are done nowadays. Agreements are oral and sealed with palm wine oblations, (and in most cases are honoured). On the other hand, such an agreement may lead to confusion and the resultant dispute will be referred to the council of elders. Here, both parties usually appear with their witnesses *(ndi-osiali)* and "lawyers" *(ndi okaikpe)*. Witnesses are those who are present when the agreements are contracted and lawyers are the elders who are the keepers of history. An elder may also take a relation of his who is a noted orator to the council of elders; to represent his views where this elder does not see himself as capable of doing so.

The attributes of a good "lawyer" are good memory, good delivery and good reputation. A good use of the precepts, proverbs and traditions would be the base of technical argument. Decisions at all levels are expected to be unanimous and as a result are not taken in haste. The fine to be imposed will depend on the gravity of the offence. Fines are paid in terms of wine, goats, fowls or sheep. In Achebe's *"Arrow of God"*, one sees a very practical example of a council session. When, in the first chapter, we saw the dispute on war policy making, which issued between Ezeulu and Nwaka. Both men were powerful and influential speakers, Ezeulu had to recline on his reputation and his position as the chief priest to convince the people to his principles while Nwaka depended on his skills as a demagogue to take the people along with him. In situations where it is difficult to arrive at a solution, the meeting usually resorts to *(Igba-Izu)*, taking council. A group of five to ten men selected at random at the suggestion of an influential elder. They withdraw from the group and discuss the pros and cons of the issue at hand. It takes a unanimous decision and return to present their decision and the reason, which informed them.

In extremely difficult cases, resort are made to the oracle and quite unlike the modern society, the gods are greatly feared and respected because of their impartial verdict and ability to inflict instant punishment on the defaulter which often come in the form of death. Oracles are shrines at which appeals are made to a god. Priest who acted as the god's mouthpiece issued the god's judgment or opinion. This is done after clients have made offerings to the god. Igbo oracles secure blessings from the gods, fortune or message from the ancestors and pronounced judgment on disputes.

Some of the Igbo oracles became nationally renowned for their impartial verdicts. They include the '*Agballa*' oracle of Awka, the '*Igweke-Ala*' oracle of Umunnoha, the '*Amadioha*' oracle of Ozuzu and the most famous of the entire, is the '*Ibini Ukpabi*' or long juju oracle at Arochukwu. It is believed that the farther the oracle is from the disputants, the more chance there is for an impartial verdict. In fact, this is why the main oracles at the main lands of the Igbo land are disregarded and never received much general recognition. Such oracles include the 'Udo', the

'Ogwugwu' and the 'Idemili'. The effectiveness and therefore the fame of an oracle lay in its apparent ability to kill by supernatural means those disobeying its verdict. Generally, such supernaturally caused death takes the form of a lingering illness, which is put down to disobedience against the oracle. A vivid example of such act by the gods is recorded in the "Arrow of God" when Ezeulu lost his most beloved son, Obika at a time when everybody in Umuaro believed that Ezeulu was not acting according to the will of his god, Ulu. They, therefore, saw the death as the god having taken sides with them and as a punishment to Ezeulu.

Oracles are also effective in killing disputants who invoke it falsely or who knowing the truth, swear to the veracity of their false claims. A litigant who invokes an oracle falsely is believed to be the guilty party, such offenders are at times killed instantly by the oracle and such is the operation of the *'Ibini Ukpabi'* oracle of Arochukwu, which made it very famous. On the whole, litigants are so convinced of a famous oracle's powers that they would tell the truth; the final result being that innocence and guilt were correctly apportioned.

On the whole, therefore, the function of the traditional government of the Igbo can be reasonably said to be legislative, executive, judiciary and religious. It provided good administration and organization to carry out its business and organized system of law and justice. It is a useful pattern of government, which provided a system connected with the peoples' religious beliefs, their relationship with one another and their business. The government is partly Theocentric and partly anthropocentric. It keeps the members of the clan together and makes it possible to call the people a community and not merely a gathering of individuals. It provided leadership.

It is necessary at this point to modify the impression that this account of Igbo traditional government might have so far given that the different clans are absolutely independent of one another. They are not really independent. Many clans are exogamous, which means that men must marry from outside the clan. Thus, one clan was bound to all the surrounding clans by inter marriage. Age grades tend to undermine the independence of a clan because people of the same age over a number of clans may hold more loyalty to their age groups than to their clans. A good masquerade or dance is repeated in different clans as a mark of respect or a goodwill visit to the clan's heads or other clans may deliberately invite the group during festivals or to teach them the dance. The practice tends to unite the clans. Again, wrestling contest, hiring of good drummers, flutters and trumpeters has strong binding effect on the clans, so do secret societies.

The title group also provides bond, which bound different clans together. The 'Ozo' title distinguishes the noble from the commoners and is a qualification for political appointment in a town. The title groups bear different names in different localities such as *'Ozo'* for Awka area, *'Ama'* for Nsukka area, *'Okpala'* *'Eze'*, *'Nze'*, *'Ume'*, *'Obi'*, *'Dim'*, *'Ichie'* etc. but they bear the same structure. All titled men are therefore politicians and may be popular or unpopular in the council of elders. They could be used politically to test the popularity of the council. The massive attendance and cheering of the people shows approval of the actions of the council of elders and serves as a vote of confidence. Poor attendance will dictate a vote of no confidence and a demand for a change or resignation. However, resignation is not easily obtainable and when such is not achieved, it has often led to dispersion. "Every man should go to become king in his own house".

The political and social culture of the Igbo society can be practically understood by an in-depth study of the novels *"Things Fall Apart"* and *"Arrow of God"*. The books especially *"Arrow of God"* are not just novels but are also documentaries, which give an account of the Igbo traditional political system and the agent of change and dispersion in the Igbo society. The Igbo generally resist any trait of central leadership or dictatorship. They resist anything that tends to undermine traditional confidence and shake the sense of common purpose and solidarity, which constitute the spirit of traditionalism. When the war waged against such traits failed, the Igbo believed on the other hand that "when the roof and walls of a house fall in, the ceiling is not left standing". *Uno anaghi adaba ghalu uko*. Everything would have fallen apart and every man retires to his tent. This is the typical result of the crisis in "Things Fall Apart" and "Arrow of God". Igbo hardly agree on one point and this had been the bane of Igbo politics and general Igbo socialism.

BIBLIOGRAPHY

ACHEBE, C. 1977, Arrow of God, Heinemann, London.

ACHEBE, C. 1983, The Trouble with Nigeria, Enugu, Fourth Dimension Publishers.

ACHEBE, C. 1985, Things Fall Apart, Lagos, Heinemann Educational Books (Nig.) Ltd.

AFIGBO, A. E. 1985, The Age of Innocence (Owerri Ministry of Information)

AFIGBO, A. E. 1972, The Warrant Chief; Indirect Rule in Southeastern Nigeria 1891-1929, London Longman Group Ltd.

AFIGBO, A. E. 1975, In, Igbo Language and Culture; Oxford University Press, Ibadan.

AFULEZI, U. N. O. 2010, Igbo 101 Facts Little Told, www Biafraland.com/Igbo, Retrieved 2012.

AKAOLISA, H. K. 2003, The Igbo Race, Origin and Controversies, Buckstar Publishers, Nigeria.

BAILEY, A. C. 2005, African Voices of the Atlantic Slave Trade: Beyond the Silence and the Shame, (ilt. ed.) Beacon Press, Boston.

BASDEN, G. T. 1966, Niger Ibos, Frank Cass, London.

BASDEN, G. T. 1966, Among Ibos of Nigeria, Frank Cass, London.

COLE, R. B. W. 1960, Kossoh Town Boy, Cambridge University Press, London.

COLEMAN, J. S. 1979, The Ibo and Yoruba Strands in Nigerian nationalism, in Robert Melson and Howard Wolpe (eds) Nigeria.

COLIS, R. 1970, Nigeria in Conflict, John West, Lagos.

CROW, H. 1970, Memoirs of the Late Captain Hugh Crow of Liverpool, London.

DAVIDSON, B. 1969, The African Genius, Little Brown and Company, Boston.

DAVIDSON, B. 1961, Old Africa Rediscovered, Victor Gollancz Ltd, London.

DIKE, K. O. 1956, Trade and Politics in the Niger Delta, Oxford Clarendon Press. London.

DIMKPA, O. 2010, Igbo Village in the United States, Daily Champion, Article in AllAfrica.com, Retrieved 2012.

ECHERUO, M. J. C. 1979, A Matter of Identity; Ministry of Information, Owerri.

EJIOFOR, L. U. 1982, Igbo Kingdoms, Power and Control, Africana Publishers Limited, Onitsha.

ENCYCLOPEDIA BRITANNICA, 2008, Bight of Biafra, Britannica Online Encyclopedia. Retrived 2008.

EQUIANO, O. 1967, Equiano's Travel; P Edwards (ed.) Heinemann, London.

EZEIFE, P. C. 2012, Ezeife Leadership Foundation, A Brief Authobiography, Abuja.

FAGE, J. D. 1962, Introduction to the History of West Africa. Cambridge University Press, London.

GREEN, M. M. 1964, Igbo Village Affair, Frank Cass, 2nd Edition, London.

HERSKOVITS, M. J. 1964, Life in the Haitian Valley, Octagon Books, Califonia.

HODDER, B. W. & UKWU, U. I. 1969, Markets in Africa, Ibadan.

HORTON, J. A. in HODGKIN, T. 1975, The Nigerian Perspective 2nd Edition, Oxford University Press, London.

IFESIEH, E. I. 1989, Religion at the Grassroots, Fourth Dimension Publishers Co Ltd, Enugu

IKE, C. O. 2009, Footprints of a Sage Edited by Uzoezie R. U. Gucks Systems Int'l, Onitsha.

ISICHEI, E. 1973, Igbo People and the Europeans; Faber and Faber Ltd, London.

ISICHEI, E. 1976, Short History of the Igbo People; Macmillan, London.

ISICHEI, E. 1977, Igbo Worlds, An Anthology of Oral Histories and Historical Descriptions, London, Macmillan

JEFFREYS, M. D. W. 1946, The Umundri Tradition of Origin, African Studies, No.15.

JONES, G. I. 1945, Agriculture and Ibo Village Planning Farm and Forest.

JONES, G. I. 1961, Ecology and Social Structure Among the North Eastern Ibo Africa, No.31.

LEITH-ROSS, S. 1939, African Women Routledge and Kegan Paul, London.

LEIRIS, M. 1965, Race & Culture, in Race, Science & Society, The Unesco Press Paris, George Allen and Unwin Ltd London.

LEONARD, A. G. 1968, The Lower Niger and its Tribes, Frank Cass, London.

LEVI-STRAUSS, C. 1965, Race and History, in Race, Science & Society, the Unesco Press Paris, George Allen and Unwin Ltd London.

LLOYD P. C. 1972, Africa in Social Change, Changing Traditional Societies in Modern World, M.d. Penguin, Baltimore.

LOVEJOY, P. E. 2000, Identity in the Shadow of Slavery, Continuum Inter. Publishing Group, London.

LOVEJOY, P. E. 2003, Trans-Atlantic Dimensions of Ethnicity in the African Diaspora, Continuum International Publishing Group, London.

MAKOZI A. O. & OJO G. J. A. 1982, History of the Catholic Church in Nigeria, Macmillan, Nigeria.

MARX, K. 1977, Genesis of Capital, Progress Publishers, Moscow.

MEEK, C. K. 1937, Law & Authority in a Nigerian Tribe; Oxford University Press, London.

MORGAN, P. D. & SEAN, H. 2004, Black Experience and the Empire. Oxford University Press, London.

NIVEN, R. 1970, The War of Nigerian Unity, 1967-1970, London.

NORTHCOTE, T. 1913, Anthropological Report on the Ibo Speaking People of Nigeria. Part 1, London, Harrison & sons.

NWABUEZE, B. 1985, The Igbo in the Contest of Modern Government And Politics in Nigeria, Owerri, Ministry of Information

NWOGA, D. 1984, The Supreme God as Stranger in Igbo Religious Thought, Hawk Press Ekwerazu.

NZE, C. 1981, Pragmatism and Traditionalism in the Concept of God in African Culture Uche, Vol. 5.

OBEGOLU E. C. 1965, Gateway to Obeledu, Ibadan.

OBIECHINA, E. 1979, The Human Dimension of History in "Arrow Of God" perspectives on Chinua Achebe, London Heinemann.

OBIKWELU, S. B. 1996, Constrains of an Igbo-Ukwu man in practicing agriculture, An oral interview, Igbo-Ukwu.

ODUMEGWU-OJUKWU, E. 1989, Because I Am Involved, Spectrum Books Ibadan.

OGBALU, F. C. & EMENANJO, E. N. 1975, Igbo Language and Culture, Oxford University Press Ibadan.

OGUEJIOFOR, J. O. 1996, Influence of Igbo Traditional Religion on the Socio-political Character of the Igbo. Fulladu Publishing Company, Nsukka.

OKEKE, S. N. 2006, Just as I Am, An Autobiography Change Publication Lagos.

OKIGBO, P. 1986, Towards a Reconstruction of the Political Economy of Igbo Civilization, Ministry of Information Owerri.

OLIVER, R. 1961, The Dawn of African History, Oxford University Press, London.

ONWUBIKO, O. 1991, African Thoughts, Religion and Culture, Enugu, Bigard Memorial Seminary.

ONWUEJEOGWU, M. A. 1975, Igbo Language and Culture, Ibadan, Oxford University Press.

ONWUEJEOGWU, M.A. 1976, The Traditional Political System of Ibusa (Ibadan, An Occasional Publication of Odinani Museum Nri, Number One.

OTTERNBERG, S. 1959, Igbo Receptivity to Change in Continuity and Change in African Culture, W. R. Bascom and Herskovit (ed.) Chicago.

OXFORD AFRICAN ENCYCLOPEDIA FOR SCHOOLS & COLLEGES, Oxford University Press 1974 Ely House London W. I.

RODNEY, W. 1972, How Europe Underdeveloped Africa, Ikenga Publishers, Enugu.

SHAW, T. 1970, Igbo-Ukwu, London.

SHAW, T. 1977, Unearthing Igbo-Ukwu, Oxford University Press, Ibadan.

TALBOT, P. A. 1926, The People of Southern Nigeria, Oxford, London.

UCHENDU, V. C. 1965, The Igbo Of South East Nigeria, New York, Holt, Richard and Winston.

UWAZIE, E. & ALBERT, I. O. 1999, Inter-Ethnic and Religious Conflict Resolution in Nigeria, Lexington Books

UWECHUE, R. 1971, Reflections on the Nigerian Civil War, Jeune Afrique Edition Paris.

UZOMA, O. 2010, Igbo People, University of Michigan Ann Arbor.

WIKIPEDIA, The Free Encyclopedia, on Emmanuel Nwude, Retrieved 2012-11-07

GLOSSARY

Afo	The third market day in Igbo culture of four market days.
Ama	A form of *ozo* title used in Nsukka area.
Ama-ala	A general council of citizens
Amaehulu	The traditional meeting arena for Igbo-Ukwu people, now is the location of the town hall.
Arrow of God	A novel by Chinua Achebe
Azudo	Literally meaning the back area of the location of the deity Udo.
Ba Kwomi	Hausa word literally meaning 'no problem' and a slogan for a carefree attitude to life.
Chukwu	The great God
Clarke	A character in Arrow of God, The British District Officer
Dim	Another form of the *ozo* title.
Efik	Igbo neighbours in the south-east
Ego	Igbo word for money.
Egwugwu	A masquerade cult in Things Fall Apart
Eke Obinikpa	A famous market in ancient Igbo society.
Eke	The first market day in Igbo culture.
Eneke-nti-oba	The Tropical Sparrow, a bird.
Eze	King or leader, Igbo word for chief.
Ezeulu	The chief priest of *Ulu*, the protagonist in Arrow of God.
Harambee	The Kenyan word for brotherhood.
Hausa-Fulani	One of the major tribes in Nigeria, found dominantly in Northern Nigeria.
Ibibio	Eastern neighbours of the Igbo
Ibini Ukpabi	An oracle in Aro Igbo communities

Ibo dance	A Haitian name for rebellious dance.
Ibo Granmoun	Haitian term meaning, Igbo take order from no one.
Ibo loa	Haitian *Vodun* Religion deity instituted by the Igbo people
Ibo	Same as Igbo, just an aberration on the term
Ibos pena'cor'a yo	A saying in Creole meaning Ibo hang themselves
Igbo-ama-eze	A saying in Igbo culture meaning that Igbo people know no kings.
Ichi	Traditional facial mark, usually very painful blood bond taken by virile people
Ichie	A higher ranking of *ozo* title
Idemili	An oracle in some Igbo communities
Igala	Northern neighbours of the Igbo
Igba-izu	Council taking
Igbo Kwenu	traditional way of saluting an Igbo gathering
Igbo	The national name as well as language of a people.
Igbo-Ukwu	The archaeological town in Igbo land.
Ikilikili	The village circle, traditionally used for social gatherings and events.
Ikwunne	One's mother's kindred or family
Ijaw	Southern Igbo neighbours in Rivers and Bayelsa State.
Ino-uwa	Re-incarnation or re-birth
Inyamili	An aberration on the Igbo sentence '*nye m mili*'
Inye-ma-ona	Association of all wives
Ise	A kind of 'Amen' use by Igbo tradition at the end of prayers
Isusu	Contributary loan scheme.
Iwa-akwa	Ceremony of Investiture for the youth
Iwanye-ogodo	Same as '*Iwai-akwa*'
Iwu-akwu	Palm business trade.

Lekou	Haitian term for an extended family compound
Nd'Igbo	Igbo people
Ndi-okaikpe	Lawyers
Ndi-osiali	Witnesses
Nkwo	The last of the four market days in Igbo.
Nnaochie	Masculine of *'nneochie'* or *'ikwunne'*
Nri	A lineage in Igbo culture with a very influential theocracy
Ntiji-egbe	Breaking or destruction of guns and fire-arm
Nwadiana	Another form for *'ikwunne'*
Nwaka	The antagonists in Arrow of God.
Nwoye	The son of Okonkwo in Things Fall Apart
Nye m mili	Give me water.
Nze	Another form of *ozo* title
Oba	Title for the feudal kings in Western Nigeria
Obejili	Scimitars, a kind of machete
Obi	Another form of the *ozo* title, used also as designation for kings in some parts.
Obiakor	A young character in Things Fall Apart
Oduche	Son of Ezeulu whom he sent to school
Ogbe	A village section
Ogoni	Southern neighbours of the Igbo people in Rivers State.
Ogwugwu	An oracle in some Igbo communities
Ohaneze Ndi Igbo	A pan Igbo organization
Oha-obodo	Same as *Ama-ala*
Okonkwo	The protagonist in Things Fall Apart
Okoye	A wealthy character in Things Fall Apart
Okpala	The primus inter pares or the head of *umunna*
Olu Ugwu Okpu	Labour center for the white man's forced labour, situated at Agulu

Ora-nwe-eze	An Igbo saying meaning that the king belongs to the people
Orie	The third market day in Igbo culture.
Oso-ahia	Market runs, market middle men
Oso-oyibo	The white man's race
Osu	The out-lawed or outcast. people offered to a deity and so are property of the deity and therefore sacrosanct
Otito dili Jesu	Praise be to Jesus
Owambe	Yoruba word literally meaning 'it is there' but used as a slogan for partying and merriment in Yoruba.
Ozo	A title that distinguishes the noble from the commoners
Sue Sue	Haitian term for *isusu* or loan scheme
Things Fall Apart	A novel by Chinua Achebe
Uda	Local spice
Udo	An oracle in some Igbo communities
Uffieh	The noble music that is dance by only the initiates of the title society.
Ujamaa	The Tanzanian word for African brotherhood popularized by Nyerere
Ulu	A divine oracle in Igbo land, used by Achebe in Arrow of God
Ume	Another version of the *ozo* title
Umuada	Association of all freeborn female citizens in a community
Umuezechima	The children of Ezechima
Umunenne	Same as '*ikwunne*'
Umunna	Large extended nuclear family
Unoka	The father of Okonkwo, a character in Things Fall Apart
Urhobo	South Western neighbours of the Igbo people in Delta State.
Yoruba	One of the major tribes in Nigeria found dominantly in Western Nigeria.

INDEX

A

African Christian 7
Akanu Ibiam   xxvi
Alvan Ikoku   xxvi
Anthropocentric 3, 103
Apprenticeships xii,20,42,69,70
Astuteness 68, 76

Agriculturist 60, 71
Akjoujk 17
America xviii, xxxv,33,34,48,61
Anthropologist xv, 5,36,57,71
Arab xxix,45,75
Autonomy 83

B

Barbados xvii, 34
Bendel   xxxii
Bight of Biafra xvii, 34
Britain xxi, xxii

Belize xviii
Biafra war xxix
Blessed Iwene Tansi xxvii
Benin Republic xxxvi

C

Cameroun xvii, xxxvi
Caribbean Island   73
Chief Emeka Anyaoku xxvii
Chief Odumegwu Ojukwu xxvii
Christendom 7
Christian Religion 7, 11, 60
Clannishness 23, 41, 42
Cuba xviii
Chukwuemeka Ezeife xi, 56

Cardinal Francis Arinze xxvii
Charles Soludo 76
Chike Obi xxvii, 76
Chinua Achebe xxvii, 41, 84
Christian Chukwu xxviii
Christoher Okigbo xxvii
Conglomerate 72
Cyprian Ekwensi xxvii
Copper 16, 17

D

Dakar   xxxiv
Denise Osadebe   xxvii
Dick Tiger xxviii, 55
Dr Nnamdi Azikiwe xxvi, 43
Dr Alex Ekwueme xxvii

Dar Fur 17
Determinism   2
Dr K. O. Mbadiwe xxvii
Dorathy Akunyili 49
Dynamism 5, 45, 89

E

Ebolanding 34
Edwin Umezeoke xxvii
Emperor Menelik II of Ethiopia xxi
Equatorial Guinea xvii
Exhibitionism 44

Egalitarianism ix, xxiv, 92
Emmanuel Ifeajuna xxviii
Enigma xi, xxi, 88
European's xiv, xxi, 7, 17, 48
Exogamous 65, 103

F

Federal Government Treasury xxx Feudalism xiv, xxiii, 35
French 33, 34   Foreign xxxi, xxxv, 46, 93, 94

G

Gabriel Okara xxvii
Guinea Bissau xxxvi

Ghana xxxvi
Granmoun 40, 82

H

H. D. Thoreau xvi
Hispaniola xviii
Heebo 33, 34
Heterogeneous 96
Harambee 20
Hausa-Fulani xxv, 24, 90, 91

Hamburg xxxiv
Herbert Macaulay 43
House of Pepple 55
Hierarchies xiv, xxv, 83
Haiti xviii, 10, 34, 40, 82, 83
Hegemony 35, 77, 79, 80, 95

I

Ibo loa xviii
Igbo slaves vii, xvii, 11,33,34,73
Individualism xi, xxiv,68,69,70,72
Islamic xxii, 9 35, 36

Ibo Granmoun 40, 82
Igbo state 21, 83
Intrinsically 46, 51
Ivory Coast xxxvi

J

Jaja of Opobo xxiii, 55
Jewish xxix
Jews ix, xxix, 45, 46
Johannesburg xxxiv
Jurisdiction 81

Jamaica xviii
Jewish Holocaust xxix
John Mikel xxviii
Julius Nyerere 20
Jos Plateau 17

K
Kanu Nwankwo xxviii
Katanga 17

Karl Marx xxi
Kingship 21, 83, 84, 85

L
Lagging 22, 63
Liverpool xxxvi

Liberia xvii
Lord Mayor of London 10

M
Major Chukwuma Nzeogwu xxvii
Mali xxxvi, 17, 19, 94
Maryland xviii
Mercenary 76
Missionaries xxiv, 5, 6, 8, 22, 37
Mauritania 17

M.I Okpara xxvi
Manchester xxxvi
Masquerade 27, 65, 97, 99, 103
Miniature 41, 83
Moshesh of Bassuto xxi
Mbonu Ojike xxvii

N
National Anthem 43
Nazi Germany 45
Ngozi Okonjo Iwuala 49, 76
Non-remunerative 80
Nwafor Orizu xxvii

Nioro 17
Ndi Okereke Onyiuke 49, 76
Niger xxxvi
Nurtured 64
NCNC 43

O
Obafemi Awolowo xxx
Obosi 37, 38, 66
Oil Rivers 18, 52
Oracular 58
Osaka xxxiv

Obasanjo O. 43
Obstinate 55
Olaudah Equiano xvii, 34, 50
Oriental mirage xxix
Owerri Division 14, 96

P
P.C. Lloyd xxiii
Peasantry xxii
Perspicacious 71
Philip Emeagwali xxviii, 76
Pretoria xxxiv

Parochial 46, 47, 81
Pend'cor'a yo xvii
Phenomenon xxiii, 38, 44
Pragmatism xi, 2, 5
Primordial 64

Prof. Kenneth Dike xxvi   Propensity 14, 43, 46, 86

Q
Quaws   48   People's Club 43

R
Royal Niger Company 37, 38   Spanish 34

S
Salomon Reinach   xxix   Sayyid Said of Zanzibar xxi
Schism   xxxii, 2   Senegal xxxvi
Shaka of Zululand and Natals xxi Shanghai xxxiv
Stephen Okechukwu xxviii, 92,94 Social Publicists xxix
Sub-Saharan Coast xxxvi   Sir Louis Mbanefo xxvii

T
Thomas Aguiyi –Ironsi xxvii   Thurstan Shaw 16, 17
Trinidad and Tobago xviii   Tripartite 90, 91
Togo xxxvi, 94   Traditional xvii, xx, 7, 9, 12, 60
Tripoli xxxiv   Trade xiii, xvii, 13,14,33,42,48
Traditional hierarchies xxv   Trans-Atlantic slave xvii, 34

U
Ujamaa   20   United kingdom xxxiv
Union 3, 43, 44, 77   Umuezechima 1, 14, 83
United States xxxiv, xxxv, xviii Umpire xv, 92

V
Virginia xvii, xviii, 34   Vodun Religion xviii

W
Warrant Chief xxiii, xxiv,38,49,81 Writers xxix, 39, 52, 92

Z
Zambia 17   Zanzibar xxi

www.ingramcontent.com/pod-product-compliance
Lightning Source LLC
Chambersburg PA
CBHW061510180526
45171CB00001B/114